TENNIS STRATEGY 101

Bill Patton

Early Reviews

Bill's Tennis Strategy 101 is the perfect read for every level of tennis player from beginner to tour level. He has captured the essence of my whole coaching philosophy. He keeps it simple, covers all the key basics, learning, strategy, mental and playing tennis as an athlete. The correct use of the eyes and footwork to produce sound stokes and the mental skills to compete successfully cannot be over emphasized.

For the teaching professional it is a perfect lesson plan to teach any student at any level. For the player it is your personal coach. It is a guide that simplifes the mysteries of an extremely challenging mental and physical sport to assist you in loving and growing in a game for your lifetime.

Ken DeHart
PTR Hall of Fame
USPTA Lifetime Achievement Award
San Jose, California

Bill Patton does it yet again. "Tennis Strategy 101" is just an outstanding guide for the novice player up to even the 3.0 or so ability range. It is easy to get bogged down with detail in describing how to do this and how to do that. But Bill holds the reader's interest with short chapters each designed to get right to the heart of the matter, whether it be general concepts of how to hit the ball and the importance of rallying or of simple strategies that are actually golden nuggets. This work serves as a great primer to help the less experienced player enjoy this great game even more. Its beauty is in its low key and simplistic approach. Personally, I can't wait for "Tennis Strategy 201." Enjoy the ride . . .

Dick Gould
Emeritus, Men's Tennis Coach & Director of Tennis
NCAA Hall of Fame Coach
Stanford University
Palo Alto, California

This is a great introduction for aspiring tennis players. Bill covers many of the basics that a person will need, to know to play competitive tennis as a new player. Bill's passion for the game and people really comes through, making this a great read for both player and teaching pro. The book is a good blue print for a player to enter the tennis world, dealing with strategies in the game as well as heartache. The game needs to grow and this will help.

Jack Broudy
Founder
Broudy Tennis
Coach and Developer of World Class Players
Denver, Colorado

Bill is one of the best and brightest minds in the game of tennis. His knowledge and insights will inspire readers of any level to immediately get out on the court and practice Bill's thoughts. He's a true leader and visionary in the tennis coaching industry!

Excellent author.... real insight, for all levels. Effective at communicating to players, coaches, and parents. Bill Patton understands the learning process, and communicates it in a practical, gracious, and humorous way.

AJ Chabria and Craig Bell
USPTA Tennis Professionals
At The Net Podcast
Dallas, Texas

Tennis is a thinking, feeling, emotional, intelligent and expressive game. Bill succinctly guides the beginner player through a philosophical, strategic and self-expressive process to become the player you are meant to be. This writing gives due diligence to a beginner player keeping a long-term mindset. The intrinsic value of performance-oriented match play coupled with the will to win is paramount to focusing on the win. Coach Patton's Tennis Strategy 101 is a blueprint for success and therefore the perfect reference tennis book every player should keep in their racquet bag.

Ron Williams
Tennis Teaching Professional USPTA
YMCA Tennis Instructor
Charleston, West Virginia

As a former competitor and current dedicated tennis coach of all levels, this book is a breath of fresh air! It is a fantastic breakdown of tennis for beginners that goes beyond the basics of technique. There are a ton of resources for advanced strategy and mental toughness specific to tennis, but it's rare to find easy-to-follow guidance for athletes just starting to get involved in the sport. The lessons are logical and clearly broken down and provide an implementable plan. This is a must read for all who are interested in taking their newfound love of hitting forehands and backhands and successfully transitioning into matchplay!

Heather Shelby Gage
National Collegiate Scholarship Association
Head Recruiting Coach Men's and Women's Tennis
High School Head Coach

Bill Patton is the coach's coach! I intended to skim through this book, but Bill's human style of writing , his unusual common sense, unwavering focus on basics, executing them meticulously, sucked me in this book. From my military training (and tennis) days, I have always been fascinated by the phrase, 'What's the difference between a narrow, painful loss and a narrow ecstatic win? If you want a straightforward, usable book that is NOT full of jargon and complications, you want this book.

Mark Jeffery
Founder of The Winning Summit,
Winning Formula and Winning Academy
Winningsummit.com
London, England

For You The Newish Tennis Player
May You Play For The Rest Of Your Life

Books
The Art of Coaching High School Tennis
The Athlete Centered Coach
Visual Training for Tennis

Courses
Four Distinct Styles of Two Handed Backhand For An
Amazing Fit
How To Play Tennis At The School Of Your Dreams,
Even If You Are Not 5 Stars
How To Train Your Players To Get To The Net

Training Aids
MBTA - Core Engagement - Foam Balls
Chute Trainer - Stroke Flow and Smoothness

Influencers
Jack Broudy - BroudyTennis.com
The Art of Winning - Styrling Strother and Dan Travis
BrainGameTennis.com - Craig O'Shannessy
Mark Jeffery - Winningsummit.com

National Collegiate Scholarship Association
Heather Shelby Gage

SportsEdTV.com
The Number One Sports Education Website In The
World

Do you want to overcome the frustration of losing matches you felt you might have been able to win?

Are you excited about the possibility of winning the close matches?

Will you find satisfaction in becoming harder to beat? Are you ready to be amazed at how you can compete at a higher level?

Welcome to tennis, new player, are you ready to build your game intelligently?

Do you want to win more matches, without having to go on a diet or more time in the gym?

The Benefits Of Tennis Strategy 101

* Protection against losing many points easily
* Make your opponent work harder
* Keys to geometry of the court
* Pressure your opponent
* The 5 Major Strategies
* Develop Your 'A' Game
* Plan to create 'B' / 'C' Game
* Play like yourself, not someone else
* Deserve to win

Serving New Players

You are new to tennis in the last few years, and you want to succeed and not fail. Many new players are leaving the game, as about 50% of new players do each year. This book has solutions for you, to keep you playing. For beginners, perhaps all the way up to the 3.5 level player, this book is meant to solve fundamental problems many people have in their strategic play.

Value Up To 3.5 NTRP, or up to 4.0 UTR

Even if you are 3.5 or over, there is a small chance this book will be of good help, even so, wait for Tennis Strategy 201, and please don't review this book, if it's not really for you, unless you see the value for the intended audience. Once you work the missing piece of your tennis puzzle, a more complete picture of your game will come into view. Some people build their puzzles starting with the outline of the object, because it's pretty easy to find the straight line edges of those pieces. This series of books is constructed similarly, as we outline the most obvious and effective, then we build one part at a time until you know the full scope of planning to win. In Tennis Strategy 202, we will then look for similar colors of puzzle pieces, beginning to match them. In 301, we get into a lot more detail to place those final bits to complete the picture of a full range of strategic and tactical options, like a 5,000 piece puzzle.

I strongly recommend that you take this book in order considering closely about each part. Read a chapter, then go play a few times with that one thought in mind. Or read the whole book in one sitting, then take each concept in order. Consider your relationship with the net. The quality of my lessons has gone way up, and the value added is greater now that I have eliminated 90% of my net errors. That same concept has helped my players to learn, since the modeling of what I do, transfers to my students they get the benefit of learning how to play better by example. Quite often, when rallying with students, there will be 5 balls in the net on their side for every one of mine (I'm still not perfect)

Next Steps

Next we take a look at the directions you hit the ball most, and if they line up with great play. Can you hit the ball where you want? If not, you really need a coach to help with that. I recommend to coaches, to share this with your students, because it can create a great framework to create conversations with your students. None of the principles in this book replace the need for having a tennis mentor in your life, and if you need a referral to a pro in your area, reach out to me and I will get some solid contacts from among the 40,000 connections I have all over the U.S, and other places around the world.

As the foundational pieces are laid, like learning the beginnings for any new skill, then we will drill down into how to better express yourself. No one expresses themselves well by not making a shot in the court... unless losing is what they want to do.

The Philosophy Of Being A Good Player

We will wrap up with some philosophical and practical advice on how to be an attractive opponent and partner. As our social circles increase, our opportunities to play will grow, at the same time, in the same way. By the end of this book you will know how to be someone who really can play tennis, and will be welcome, to go to higher levels. I'm excited to hear your testimonials and reviews. Keep in mind, this book is really targeted mostly to the 2.5 player, and those in that range. 101 serves as a review up to 3.5 level play, but Tennis Strategy 201 will be target mainly to the 3.0 to 4.0 player, giving them an edge in competition. The 301 class will help 4.0 and above players dial in their strategies and tactics, with enough detail to overcome today's tough match up and move to 4.5 and beyond. Our sport really needs more players to get up to the 4.5 and 5.0 player, let it be you!

Now, let's get started with understanding the foundational truths that will make you harder to beat, help you win the close matches, and gain on the next level ahead of you. I'm excited for how your results are going to improve. Are you ready to discuss what tennis means to you? Read on!

Chapter One

How Do I Build
A Winning Tennis Game?

Begin with the end in mind. ~ Steven Covey

Sadly, a large degree of tennis players surrender their intelligence in a tennis match. Is that you? Do you look back on matches and wonder why you didn't think to do something better? This book will solve many of those problems for you. People get so caught up in short-term outcomes, that they fail to see the bigger picture. This book will give you the solution to looking at the overall victory of the war of a few sets, instead of getting discouraged by losing a battle here and there. Also, you will become a wise general of your tennis combat.

We start your awesome journey as a tennis player with a quick overview of the mindset you need to compete, play smart and improve.

There is a lot of orthodox belief spread at clubs, parks, on USTA teams, and with many tennis coaches. The conventional wisdom they offer usually results in players getting stuck at certain levels of play, especially at 3.0, 3.5, and 4.0. In sharp contrast, I have enjoyed coaching seemingly under-talented players, with less skill, to win against those who seem superior, in almost every way. This guidebook will help point you in the direction of smarter play, and higher places on the ladder. This isn't winning ugly or mastering anything, looking for your talent code, grit, or any other contemporary idea, instead of using basic logic, with an understanding of how to win a tennis match. The best news is that the answers are very simple.

The simplest solution is usually the best.
~ Albert Einstein.

You can find simple ways to play smart, and use subtle truths that others gloss over. Think about how you are going to feel when you do the basics so well, that you become much harder to beat. I marvel at how many times people try some sophisticated strategy and techniques but haven't even learned the fundamentals very well. It's also going to be relatively painless, to learn the principles here, except the pain you might feel from having not understood them earlier. Get ready to play the mental tennis, that works for you.

Performance = Potential - Interference

If you remove all interference, your performance will meet its potential. Suffer along with the rest of us, who are not quite perfect yet, but go forward to remove the largest manageable problems, that get in the way of having your best performance. This formula comes from, Tim Gallwey, author of the Inner Game of Tennis, and founder of the Inner Game coaching franchise.

When we get to the end of this work, you will understand and have some great action items to lose fewer points, win more points, and what your ultimate goals can be as a player.

One of the ways you can remove impediments is to stop making the same mistakes again and again. Identify your one most common mistake, identify the root cause with the help of your coach, and have fun rooting it out. Think how great you are going to feel when you no longer hit 50 balls into the net in competition.

Ultimate Goals

A mistake that is all too common is that players try to play like someone else. People often try to imitate someone with whom they share almost nothing in terms of physicality, mentality, or spirit. So, if you are 5'2 and 110 pounds with 12" arms, please stop trying to play like Nadal. On the other hand if you are 6' and 180 pounds and have 20" biceps, then give it a go. In the final analysis, your best way to play is like YOU!

Common Fundamentals Among The Greats

Of course, there are many great commonalities among the great players, they do many things the same way, but Federer does not play like Djokovic, who also does not play like Nadal. Barty doesn't play like Serena Williams or Peng Shuai. On the other hand, if there is a player with whom you share a similar physique, personality, or mentality, they may serve as a good model for you. I once had a player who did everything as though he was mimicking Federer and he played well. Another player would one day hit a Fed forehand, and a few days later it was Nadal, He would hit a Djokovic backhand, then another day it was a different player. He would try a Roddick serve, then a different one. I tried to help him understand that "I want to help you play like you!" Frustrated, he left, and to my knowledge has never exceeded 3.5, although I thought he had the athleticism to become a 5.0 NTRP Level Player.

Conclusion

No matter who you are, and how you express yourself, you will never win a point when you hit the ball into the net. There are certain immutable laws of tennis, that when you violate them, you create friction, you increase problems, and thus play below your potential.

It's a brain game you are playing here, so use it. There is an art to winning, and while I recommend reading The Inner Game of Tennis, 7 Habits To Enter Your Play State, Match Play And The Spin Of The Ball In The 21st Century, this book is not at all about the mental game and concentration, it's simply about hitting the ball where you want it to land. You will also have an opportunity to learn, to avoid placing the ball where you don't want it to go. We will also look at the risk/reward ratio, how that guides your decision-making, your reactions to success and failure, and how you move forward in a match toward the win. I am very confident that there will be a close match you win, that you formerly used to lose, that will be an exciting one for you. I can't wait to hear about it!

Geometric Building Blocks

You add before you subtract, you add before you multiply,

then it's on to exponents, and radicals, and beyond. Take each thing as a foundational piece, so that you can place the rest of your game on a rock-solid foundation. When you do this, you can win some matches, even when you are not playing your best. If you are failing, at the 1+1 math, in your game, then working more complex formulas will not save you. Players up to 3.5 can find some wisdom here, open your mind to the basics. Tennis Strategy 201, will cover a range from 2.5 to 4.0, and then 301 in this series will be for the 4.0 and above crowd, those that want to play at 4.5 and above.

Getting Grounded In Reality

As a word of warning to the grandiose readers out there, all the strategies in the world will not help you, when you are completely overmatched. So if you imagine that you are a 2.5 that will now beat your club pro, then you have another thing coming. A mental mistake that is made often is speculating on their ranking. I hear often 'My UTR is x, but would be x+1, if…". So come back down to earth, your rating is your rating, and everyone faces adversity, so if everyone added one to their rating, it would all be equal anyway. If you are playing someone who is one full UTR rating point above you, all you can hope for is to get a few games, unless they are hurt, sick or grieving. Even so, play good strategy, be a tough person to beat, and you can use those experiences to beat other people later and gain a measure of satisfaction. You also are not going to have a lot of fun and satisfaction if you are unwittingly beating yourself. We will begin by placing things in proper perspective, then starting to remove the impediments to winning.

Chapter Two

Where Do I Stand With Other Players?

So, you want to play tennis? This first chapter is about the strategies you can use simply to play more tennis. It's good to start with understanding the people who play the sport. You might be surprised to learn how most people engage with the sport. About 20 years ago I heard some data that was shared by OncourtOffcourt guru Joe Dinoffer. The data seems to indicate that about 80% of people who want to play tennis only really want to rally for a while, 30-45 minutes, work up a sweat, then head home. They just want to have a cross-training workout or get enough exercise to stay alive.

The Social Set

Another big chunk of players, perhaps 15% of them want to play a social set of mostly doubles, or singles in a pinch, to see their friends, have fun, and maybe a little trash talk.

The Lunatic Fringe

Somewhere around 5% or less want to compete to win,

want to be on a team, and are driven to play at the highest level they can play. Some of them want to sandbag down to the lowest level so that they can have relative success compared to players that they are truly better than. It's up to you if you want to join this group, but if you don't you can still play with these people. Among these people are those who have it in perspective, they understand that it's just a game, but they will give their all. A smaller group have their egos so wrapped up in it, that you can see how much emotional energy to put into wins and losses.

Know What You Are Getting Into

You may want to interview the people you are going to play, to see if it's a good fit for you. When you are finding new people to play at your club, at a park, or wherever you play, take some time to get to know the other people and what they like to do, don't assume that their goals are the same as yours, but your values don't need to completely align for you to have a good hit, a set, or be teammates.

Unwritten Rules (Until Now)

One of the unwritten rules of our sport is that if you can rally, people will want to play with you, but if you can't they won't want to play. In addition, if you can play a competent match, you don't double fault 20 times and make your returns, then they might invite you to play again, but if you are not a challenge or a workout, then they will make excuses to avoid playing with you. Don't take any of this personally, simply work on your game.

Some may say, "You need to be more consistent." What does that mean exactly? Find out in the next chapter.

Chapter Three

What Does 'Consistency' Mean?

A foolish consistency is the
hob goblin of small minds. ~ Emerson

The advent of Covid-19 in 2020 has seen a huge influx of players into tennis. Tennis is well noted as the safest sport you can play for disease transmission. A Danish study has shown that tennis players live on average 11 years longer than those who don't play. Now that you are playing, raising or coaching new players, it's vital that you gain a thorough understanding of how to play. You want to have fun, improve and win! The problem is that you most likely will run into some damaging dogma, that has permeated the game. When perpetuated, these off the mark, but commonly held beliefs frequently leads to frustration. For too many, they then quit the sport, because they didn't find great solutions. Don't let that happen to you! Start with a mindset for growing success.

What Is The Value Of Consistency?

A large percentage of the people who come to me for a first lesson say that they want to learn to be more consistent. For many years, I thought this would be a helpful aspect of tennis, because I had obsessed about the same thing myself, and had been harangued by coaches, or team captains, even when I won my match. I have now learned that the C word is not as important as I once thought.

Think for a moment, how many times have you heard someone say "I am happy with my consistency". I'm guessing that it has happened rarely, or maybe never. So, if people are never really happy with their consistency, then why do we work on something that does not allow for success? The short answer is that we should spend our time thinking on what does help us take the next steps of improvement.

The Sun Revolves Around The Earth

Before you vilify me as a tennis heretic, read on, because it's a simple shift of mindset that creates a massive difference. There was a time that people thought the sun revolved around the earth, and when it was proposed otherwise, that person was deemed a heretic. I'm saying that our game should not revolve around consistency in the way most people do, but what you will find is that it's not a big leap to change your mind just a little to play with more smarts, and less self-criticism.

The Subtle Shift

I'm not saying play recklessly, but am suggesting a subtle

shift in the emphasis in your mindset. Instead of signing up for the misery of a subjective hell of trying for making every single shot, beating yourself up every time you miss, try using objectives that are more effective. As you know any missed shot is a symptom of a lack of consistency, instead go for a risk : reward ratio. You take some measure of risk on every shot anyway, so why not also reap better rewards? Sounds good? Let's get started.

> Every missed shot is a sign of not being
> consistent, to those who think that way.

Do You Want To Make More Shots?

I want you and your players to make more shots, we want them to learn to take calculated risks, to be assertive, to take control of the match. Unless, of course, you want to live in the fear of missing, but that's your choice, and you should probably stop reading any further. Even if you try to never make an error, you still will, and you will soon, as at most 45% of points go longer than 5 shots, and at many levels only 25% of points last that long. If you are training to never miss, but your opponent is training to make something happen, that player has the advantage, and they won't spend as much time in self criticism.

Playing Keep Away

Frank Giampaolo, a great friend, and a top coach who works with amazing players, told me a story about working with a national training camp. Players were split into equal playing ability groups. One group was told to rally with each other, and be consistent, while the other group was trained for the same amount of days to keep the ball away from their opponent. When the groups were brought back together for a competition, one group against the other, the players who trained to play 'keep away' won decisively.

Finding The Place Of Tension

From the beginning, realize that there is a risk to every shot. The first big pain you will want to relieve, is that of hitting into the net. Reduce risks first, then increase rewards. Finding the place of tension, where you get the most pay off for your shot making, without dramatically increasing errors is the way to win.

Big Data

In global data for all matches combined, 70% of all errors go into the net. When you are mindful to have great net clearance of 2' to 3' or more, you can reduce that number to 35% or much lower. More often than not, your opponent will not be aware of that data in any way, so you can enjoy their netted shots.

More Benefits To Come

There are numerous benefits to good net clearance, but we will break that down in the next chapter. We then will move on to the importance of knowing how to set your points up crosscourt, or down the middle. From there, examine a few more issues that cause errors, take a look at how to cause them in our opponents, then finish up with how to play like yourself.

Discover Your Way To Play

Are you going to allow someone else tell you how to express yourself? I not here to tell you want to do, but I can offer suggestions of where you can discover how to play like you. I will offer some options, and show you why a fairly finite field of choices are realistic. If someone can show me another option, I'm open to it. The benefits of doing a little self-evaluation, to discover which style of play really suits you, can be the difference between being free to play, and feeling forced into a mold that you don't like. As though an artist, you still have to learn to draw straight lines and perfect circles. If you compare tennis to being a musician, you will need to learn to play your scales. You have to study some logic, if you want to be lawyer, and you better know how to read, if you are going to be a teacher. You get my point.

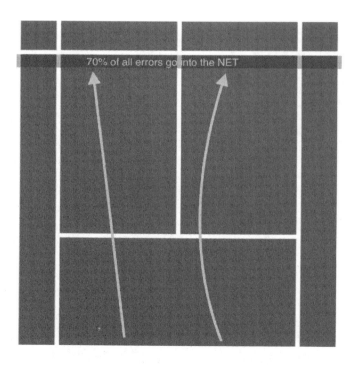

The net is there for everyone, and it does not matter what

style you play. The net does not care what is on your mind, if you hit into it, you lose the point every time. If you want to make more shots, placing the ball where you want, it's always NOT going to be in the net. This is the magic, do what you want, and remember what you want. You want to hit the ball where you want. This is why the beginning chapters of this book are about the foundational thoughts, for you to reduce the amount of errors you make, then onward to making more kinds of shots, having longer rallies, learning to be happy about it. Don't obsess about every miss, but do learn from it, so that you can miss less often. Rafa Nadal, who at times, has been the lowest risk player on the tour, will still make 7-10 unforced errors per set. In a particularly sterling performance, he might make only 3. You will probably make a few more, accept that.

You will eventually need to learn how and when to go for your shots!

Chapter Four

Are There Secrets To Making More Shots?

More errors mean less consistency,
Fewer errors mean more consistency,
No errors are not realistic,
because everyone makes them.

You see a lot of amazing marketing, in tennis, that says, "Learn the X number secrets of..." and it works very well. The only way for something to be a secret is to not know it already. I'm pretty sure that some of these concepts might count as being secrets because presented this way, it will be brand new to you. In fact, until people come to understand what I am saying here, they are usually shocked, having a little cognitive dissonance, so I want to prepare you for that. It can be upsetting to have some basic assumptions questioned. Sometimes, people can be a bit dismissive, because they think they know better, but that's not you. Still, there will be some players who need a little time to think, so that they can get through the stages of truth.

Remember the stages of truth:
1. Ridicule.
2. Vehement Argument
3. Acceptance
4. No memory of 1. and 2.

What Do You Want To Achieve?

In achieving that holy grail of consistency, what is the ultimate goal that you desire? How will you know when you achieve the desired result? Do you want to know when you have succeeded? Do you constantly want to feel like a failure? Will every error eat at you, as evidence of not having achieved anything? This chapter will give you a framework, by which you can measure your progress, and customize that improvement for yourself. You will gain skills, avoid repeated failure, and find that more close matches are winnable. You can begin to play better with higher-level opponents. Your frustration and anxiety will decrease, and your success and joy will increase.

Conventional Wisdom Of Consistency

Consistency is one of the most commonly used words in tennis play. Players berate themselves, and others, for not doing well enough, in what they feel is a vital aspect of the game. Among players who are 3.0 and above, in the first lessons, it's almost universal, that the player comes to me seeking to be more consistent. Players up to 2.5 have not really been exposed to the term yet, so they haven't had a chance to become miserable yet. Usually, other players will infect you with the term, like a virus that creates unhappiness. Instead, let's start with being a joyful tennis player. Take the inoculation (no needles required) against self-doubt and recrimination. Hold on tight.

The only way for something to be a secret,
is for you not to know it already.

Relax, Have Fun, Make Shots

So then, if players are never happy, or almost never happy with how consistent they are, then why would you make that your aim? It doesn't make sense. Instead, redirect your thinking, to something that will fill you with a sense of accomplishment, and the growing confidence that comes with it. My first lessons, with players I am meeting for the first time, begin with getting relaxed, having fun, and learning what is most important.

People plant, grow, and water an impossible
standard in their minds, and thus failing it again
and again, are ripe to drop off the tennis tree.

We start by making easy shots, developing success, then increasing the challenge level to more and more difficult shots. We also don't obsess on missed balls but remember the ones we like to reproduce them. Isn't that what you want? We also work on placing them, where you want to hit them. To hit balls where you want, you have to risk to some degree of missing your target. That means you have to accept that you are not going to make every ball. Once you reach that conclusion, you don't have to sign up for the regular self-criticisms, concluding that every ball missed is evidence of not having the C-word. You can accept that you are not perfect, just like me and everyone else who plays this game.

Developing Your Plays

As you progress, you will want to set up and execute plays, where you hit shot combinations, with a slightly elevated element of risk, but also higher rewards in the long term. Consider that even the most conservative defensive players who specialize in not missing will still have slightly under 10 unforced errors per set. Of course, it's a subjective judgment, how those mistakes are judged, but that's 3-9 points where you missed a shot you should have made.

A Very Basic Play

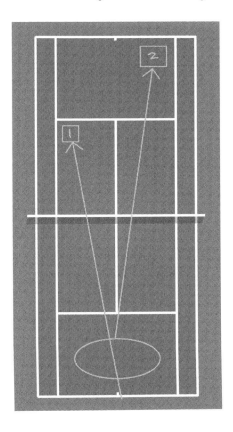

Acceptable Amounts Of Errors

A good friend of mine played Andre Agassi, Pete Sampras, and Michael Chang in the juniors in Southern California. He lost to Sampras 7-5, 6-4, then he lost to Andre Agassi 6-2, 6-1. When he played Michael Chang, he only won three points because Chang double-faulted one time, and then missed lines by 'that much (fingers very close together)', twice, so those were the three points that he won against Chang. Showing that even an extremely dominant performance will have some unforced errors in it.

Nothing Ventured, Nothing Gained

Go For Some Strong First Serves

If you never go for a strong first serve, you might maximize your serve percentage, but then you will miss out on the benefits of using the most frequently used offensive shot in the game. There is an advantage to be gained in taking the aggression out on them. On the other hand, since the most common rally length is 1 shot, meaning the serve goes in, and is not returned, you certainly don't want to compromise your first serve percentage seriously. It's all about balance. When you go for a big first serve, you might make that 50% of the time or less, that's ok as long as you win a high percentage of those points, otherwise, you will have to hit so many more second serves, risking more double faults, using up a lot more energy.

Venture To The Net

Coming to the net gives an overall winning percentage of 63%, overall. That means 37% of points you don't win at the net. Will you let that deter you? There will be a few missed approach shots, a few missed volleys, and overheads. Serving and volleying seems like a higher risk, but if you spend some time learning how to do it, and give it a little practice, it can lead to a 67% win percentage. Still, one-third of the points will be lost, and a high percentage of those will be from errors, but if you don't venture, nothing is gained. Be ok with that, losing the one point to win two.

Know What Is Most Likely To Happen At Net

When you go to the net, the most common thing that wins the point is that the opponent misses a passing shot, which means you did not even have to make that volley. Keep track of those. The next thing that happens often is you miss a volley, but that is followed closely by, you making a winning volley, and finally by the opponent making a winning passing shot. The point here being fully made, is that you have to be able to tolerate some errors, if you want to make your opponent, make more of them. That's why it's important to understand the difference between Forced Errors, and Unforced Errors, and what causes them.

You will become more successful in your ventures when you can better place the ball, where you want it to go. That is the topic of the next chapter, how to make more shots.

Chapter Five

Where Do I Want The Ball To Go?

Every shot should have a target.
~ Tennis maxim

Recently I was on the court with a high-ranking military officer. This person said, "If I make a mistake, people die." This is a very successful person. They are trying to rediscover confidence, in a return to competitive tennis, after a long layoff. We were having her learn to hit 5 shots in a row to a small target area. In the short term, quite a few shots went in every direction, except in the target area of my racquet. I would feed her a ball, and her shot was supposed to go where I could easily volley it back without having to move too much. After a short while, she put a ball right on my strings, but then that success leads to quite a few misses, before doing it again. Then finally, she made two in a row, followed by a lengthy backslide, brought on by the excitement, and pressure to do it again. She repeated two in a row a few times before we stopped to find out what was the issue with getting to three. Then she was able to make three out of four, and then four out of five, before finally doing three in a row.

Shortly, she could do six out of seven, but not more than three, before finally doing five in a row. The point here is, that you will have to understand the mental and emotional processes of allowing yourself to succeed. Sometimes it feels like the internal dialogue of the player is "Why can't I do it again, what is wrong with me?"

Targets Are New Things?

We had spent a little time on task working on her forehand in the vacuum of having a target, so the shot was warmed up, but now her mentality needed a stretch. Prior to our work on this, she only had a vague understanding of where she wanted to hit shots. This is because she had not attempted to hit a small target area before this time. Previously her only thought about this shot was to "get it in the court", which is not specific enough to execute a strategy in a live match. This is also a core thought behind the so-called 'consistent player'.

Are you really going to beat
yourself up every time you miss?

Now with a specific objective in mind, she is able to hit very small targets on the court, more regularly. This highlights another weakness of the generic understanding of consistency. Shots that are 'in' are considered 'good' and those that are 'out' are 'bad'. This kind of thinking allows people to accept very poor shot-making, in the name of shots, that make it inside the court. That level of thinking, also assigns a negative value, to a deep crosscourt shot, that you can make nine out of ten times because you missed one time. Even though the nine shots made in drive a high winning percentage of points. We need to readjust our thinking about what percentage of shots we need to make.

What Is A Missed Shot Worth?

Look at Federer, look at how many balls he will mishit in a match, he'll completely shank one or two balls and he just walks away as though it's no big deal. The bottom line: work not obsess so much about missing a few balls here and there, as the emotional toll it takes can wreck your confidence, just get back to preparing well for the next point, and keep going for your best targets.

Get The Most Out Each Miss

When you do miss, objectively observe what has happened, where did the ball go, where did you want to go, what was the problem, and how can you correct it?

Work on making more shots in a row in the court, getting the ball up and over, deep cross-court, and/or too different places that challenge your opponent. We are going to flesh out each of those things in the coming chapters. Understand risk:reward ratio, because even when you're playing the safest shot you possibly can, you're still going to miss one in twenty shots. Are you going to beat yourself up every time you're missing?   We will begin by learning the most important way to reduce errors of one kind while accepting errors of another.

Chapter Six

What Is The Biggest Obstacle To Winning?

Tennis is a lifting game. ~ Vic Braden

70% of all errors are in the net. 2/3 of all points played end in errors. Be the one who gets the ball over the net! If you are a new tennis player, or coaching new players, learning this primary objective can be the difference, between staying in the game and leaving it frustrated. If knowing this, you train to get the ball up and over, allowing for a marginal increase in the percentage of balls that go long or wide, then you gain an edge, over those who are unwittingly failing, to clear the only obstacle in the sport. Read that last sentence over again.

What percentage of tennis shots are hit upward?

Net Clearance Is A Fundamental

We have already discussed how to eliminate errors in the name of the game. The top players in the world also do this, and their average groundstroke rally shots are struck 2.5' to over 3' over the net.   Learning proper net clearance is important. One theory I have, as for why players attempt to hit shots fast and low, is that they watch tennis on a two-dimensional screen. It's easy to come away, with the impression, that the ball whizzes very close to the net, a danger that makes it look exciting. When you see tennis live in person, in three dimensions, you realize, that the ball, is not as low to the net, as you thought, from watching on a screen.

One thing we know for sure is, if you hit in the net, you lose the point immediately, except on a first serve.

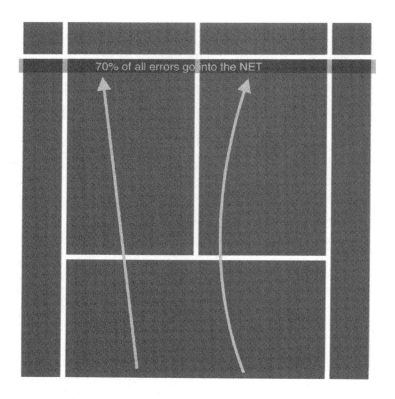

70% of all errors go into the NET

Cutting Net Errors In Half

Let's say that you cut your errors, in the net, in half, so that you are reducing that kind of error to 35% instead of the average of 70%. Once you do that, there will be a slight increase, in the number of errors, where the ball goes long by X% and the ones that go wide by X%. That means you will have reduced your errors by 35-2X%, so as long as you don't blast many balls long, you gain a lot of made shots. The greater benefit is that you will also keep the ball deep, and make better use of angles. You gain three new advantages, just by reducing the percentage of balls in the net!

The first job of the tennis player is to get the ball over the net. Balls in the net are NEVER called in, but balls an inch long get called in frequently.

This Method Is Not Often Taught

The problem is that this objective is not reflected in the way people learn and teach tennis. Quite a few new players become obsessed with topspin because that's what coaches teach, maybe a little too early. In the early going, topspin can lead to even more balls in the net, because of mistimed shots, and the fact that topspin shots land shorter. Reflect on the quote at the top of the page, by Vic Braden, "Tennis is a lifting game". The relative angle of your racquet face, should be set, to get good net clearance, sending the ball a few feet over the net, and deep in the court.

Chapter Seven

Why Do Players Value The Wrong Shots?

One thing we see all over the tennis world is an obsession with technique, but we don't see as much interest, in learning how to win a tennis match. There is a misplaced assumption, that a player with better technique, is fully equipped, to win a match, against someone with inferior strokes. In reality, how well you get the ball up and over the net, is far more dependent on how well you move to the ball. Getting into position to receive the ball cleanly, near the middle of your strings is just as important, if not more important than how you swing. The angle you create with your racquet face is just as important, for sending the ball in a nice arc beyond the obstacle.

Pushers win, everyone who presumes themselvesto be superior to them is frustrated to against that style.

They Know That!

What Is Really Important?

Instead of learning how to play fundamentally sound strategy, people fantasize about hitting their forehands like Nadal or Federer, and their backhands like Djokovic, even if it goes in the net more often, and never reaches their opponent. Even if that particular shot does not fit with how they are predisposed to hit. Don't get me wrong, you need solid stroking fundamentals, but you don't need to have perfected world-class strokes in order to win. How will you assert you're control of the match if the opponent doesn't have to hit your shot back?

There are some amusing benefits to hitting the ball over the net:

> **1. You don't have to pick the ball up.**
> **2. You don't have to do the "walk of shame".**
> **3. Sometimes the ball is called in...**

Upward Bound

I ask my players to guess what percentage of shots are hit upward. They usually start guessing within the 50% to 70% range, and I tell them "higher, higher" until they get in the 90% range, then I tell them... 99% of all shots are actually hit upward initially. All of my players think this way until they learn the true stat, so there is a wide discrepancy between what they perceive and the reality of balls that travel upward. This partially explains why so many go in the net. The exceptions to this rule are very high volleys, and overheads from very close to the net. I like to show my players a volley, and how it looks like it's dropping, and penetrating the court, their attention is on the outcome of the shot, not the origin of it. Then I bring their attention, to the initial flight of the ball, off my string bed. They clearly can see, the ball is rising slightly at first, thus making it an upward shot. Again, Vic Braden shared that when you hit an overhead from the baseline, with an 8 degree upward tilt on the face of the racquet, the ball will make it to the opposite baseline. Getting good depth on overheads can dramatically increase their effectiveness. Even when you drop a shot, you can think of it as a very tiny lob, up and over, and the more vertical your drop shot, the closer the second bounce is to the net.

Prefer Your Errors Deep, Rationalizing

Rationalizing is not always bad, but you have to be right. You have to have some level of acceptance. It's true that when you are going for more depth, the ball might go out long or wide, that's the risk you take. But now gravity is your friend keeping the ball in and you will be surprised how many shots stay in, as opposed to being surprised at how many balls go in the net when you are not doing for depth.

Very Long Shots Are OK In The Short Run

Even if you hit the ball 10 feet out, at least you are being aggressive! The problem is that inexperienced players overreact to balls that go long so that when they hit one 10 feet out, they can follow that up with a ball that is 15 feet short in the court, but that's not going to help to have the wild differences in your shots. You want to hit the ball a bit shorter. Instead, it's better to adjust by degrees, so you may hit a ball only 5 feet out, followed by 3 feet, until you can get your ball to land in the last 5 feet of the court. Once you get the range, you are good to go, for most of the rest of the match. Setting the tone with depth, then reducing it is easier than starting tight with short shots and trying to open it up for more depth. The deeper shots push your opponents back, forcing them to hit into the net more often. This is how you win the field position battle of tennis, pushing them back, while you get to play closer. So, you have to learn to be ok with a few very deep shots early in the match, to help set the tone for the rest of it.

Placing Value On Depth

I sometimes play a game with my players where they have to collect a certain amount of points. You can see that the best thing you can do here is not worried about hitting deep because in the game you won't lose any points, and when you learn to shorten your shots, they will

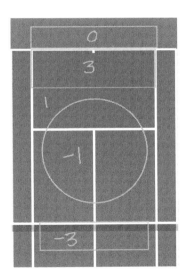

Underlining The Obsession With Missing

Players who simply obsess about any miss, are unable to rationalize a few long balls, they can't objectively see the advantages of where you miss, and how that will help when you learn to get the proper range on the depth.

> *When you look at the net, then you will hit into it,*
> *but when you look beyond it to the target*
> *you want to hit, then you are much more likely*
> *to beat the first enemy.*

Your first job is to learn to hit over the net, all other considerations are secondary. You will beat some players with fancier strokes if you do this. Then you will be ready to take on a slightly more complicated task of determining which kind of errors are being made, and how do you decide what to call them.

Chapter Eight

How Do I Interpret Different Errors?

Tennis matches are won by forcing errors.
~ Bill Jacobsen, Founder of CompuTennis, 1989

I started with tennis data in the mid-1980s as my girlfriend, now wife charted my matches. Later, I ran CompuTennis on an Epson laptop in 1989 and 1990 for Cal State East Bay Men's Tennis Team a perennial Division II powerhouse. The ability to split out data from deuce to ad courts was an amazing tool for on-court coaching. As a championship high school coach, I taught my Junior Varsity players how to chart the Varsity. Also being able to tell a player to continue to be aggressive, because while their winners were low, but the errors they were forcing were high, matches were won! The problem with understanding errors is that dividing between forced and unforced errors is a subjective process. A wide range of subjective judgments from person to person exists according to their particular bias.

A great working definition is that an error is simply a

missed shot. An unforced error is a stroke you would naturally be expected to make if you took the most conservative approach to it. Forced errors, give credit to the opponent, for having made a shot, placing you under significant enough pressure, that we would not expect that you make that shot very often. The trouble is in the gray area in between those two ideas. What you want to avoid is excuse-making. In order for it to be a forced error, the opponent must have hit the ball very hard, with a lot of spins, at the player, or made them run a significant distance. Who determines, who caused the error? We will dig a little deeper into that, but ultimately it's YOUR standard for how you interpret yours and your opponent's errors that needs to be well-honed, and reliable.

The human factor of subjective judgment makes relying on stats taken by a person somewhat unreliable. First serves, points won, and net points are hard and fast. Unforced and forced errors are subjectively judged.

The Psychology Of Error Interpretation

Everyone has different standards for defining the difference between the two types of errors. Even winners come in different types, the 'excuse me' shot. that the opponent doesn't touch, and the intentional well placed offense, that they can't touch. There are times that you go for a forcing shot, and the ball just seems to be a bit better than you planned, it becomes a winner. Maybe you mishit a shot, that barely goes over the net, for an accidental drop shot winner, it still counts in the winner column, regardless of your feelings about it. Our favorites are the winners, where you have an open court, go for the finish, and make it.

Winners

A winner is a winner, the ball bounced twice and the other player did not get it. Simple. But, unforced errors are subject to the particular judgments, of the person doing the charting. Do they have a relationship with one player or the other? Do they have extremely high or low standards for what is expected? Are they kind-hearted, or harsh? The bias of the person will color the datasheet. You need to know the person taking the stats for them to be understandable. SwingVision is a great alternative because it's A.I. driven, and through machine learning, it comes up with data that is free of human judgment. Even when the calibration is off, you can still gain valuable insight into your play.

Serves, Returns, Points Won, Going To Net

If someone is simply charting whether a serve went in or not, and if the point was won, then that removes the subjectivity. When certain criteria for whether a player went to the net is established, for instance, if both of their feet were in the service box, then you can easily mark that as well. These things are not open to interpretation and can be quite helpful. Also, where balls landed out can be marked on the sheet, but that also takes a keen eye. To help the person chart, be sure to call the score every time so that they know if close balls were in or out. Make calls that are easy for the charter to see or hear.

Deeper Understanding Forced / Unforced

My definition of unforced error is any shot that you could and should make. Any attempt where you are on balance, in position, have your racket on the ball, you should be able to make that shot. There are also many shots you can make, even when you barely get the edge of your racquet behind the ball. If you don't make the shot, that is unforced.

Shot Selection Errors

It's also an unforced error when you go for too much power, or angle on a shot, thus missing it long or wide. Keep in mind, not all unforced errors are the same, some unforced errors are acceptable when they are part of becoming a more assertive player with controlled aggression. We will break that down more in Tennis Strategy 201.

Learn to objectively observe the difference between errors, and give your opponent credit for good shots made, and you can reduce the pressure you feel.

Any time you choose the wrong shot, or change your mind in the middle and thus miss, that is also unforced. No one made you do that. If you could have lobbed on that shot and made it, instead of the shot you chose, then it's unforced. Learn to recognize defensive situations and play accordingly.

Errors Of Impatience

If you miss because you were impatient, that can be borderline, because the other player played more patiently, and they forced you beyond your comfort zone for rallying. If you make a bad decision to suddenly go for a winner, then that is an unforced error.

Forced Errors

When the ball comes much higher than you like, that is also one of the most common difficulties of the player below 3.5. The less experience you have, the more likely it is that you will have difficulty with high balls. Get a lesson on that!

Whenever the other player gets you off balance, out of position, or in a place of bad posture, then it's a good chance it was a forced error, but don't use it as an excuse. You can still make shots when off-balance, out of position, and in bad posture. Learn to lob when you are in a bad place, as you can get out of trouble.

Chapter Nine

What Is The Best Way To React To Errors?

To thine own self be true.
~ Polonius

Who you are, how anxious you are, and how you deal with adversity has a lot to do with how you will interpret your errors and those of others. Some people almost exclusively blame themselves for every bad thing that happens. Other people seem to often blame someone else for their problems. Most people fall somewhere in the middle, majoring in one and minoring in the other. The better we do at objectively observing what is really happening, the better. Dropping the blame and the shame, and simply taking responsibility for your misses can take you a long way.

Perfectionism

There is also a continuum of perfectionism. On one end of the scale, you have those who were raised with the idea, that if they got 99% right on a test, their parents won't know why they missed one. Then you have people who were perfectly happy getting C's in school, and if they got an A or B, they were subject to teasing for buying into school.

Where ever the ball goes, you were
the one who hit it to that place.

The first group agonizes over every miss, and the second group might not mind a truckload of errors, as long as they hit a few winners. The perfectionistic may feel bad even when their opponent hits a 90 MPH shot into the corner, even so, they feel like they should have had it. The other people who make a ton of errors might blame something else, like gravity for not keeping their ball in the court. They have many excuses and can explain easily why a certain shot that was missed was an outlier and not their fault.

Self-judgment

In general, I find that most players wince, cuss under their breath, and generally display anger, disappointment, frustration, and a general lack of acceptance for any missed shot. Most people blame themselves and react emotionally to every single missed shot. Children might miss six straight shots, make the seventh one, and be excited. Adults often might make six straight shots miss the seventh and express frustration. Let go of self-judgment and you might find you enjoy the game more deeply.

Subjectivity

Subjective judgments given to 'bad' shots are part of the problem in and of itself. Move away from subjectivity and emotion to judge your shots. Try to look simply at 'what is' and 'what happened, rather than placing blame or taking credit. Emotional reactions to 'good' shots can be an equal-sized problem. It's common that after making a nice shot, players feel pressure to do it again. Instead, just enjoy your play and move on to the next one. Each ball coming toward you presents a unique problem. Master Pro Ken DeHart who has reviewed this book says, "Every ball is a question, do you have the answer?" Ken is a great coach, and his influence can be seen in this work. So, coming to a place of simply observing what is, can be the best antidote to this up and down rollercoaster of emotion. The better you can leave all judgments aside and stay in the moment, the more fun you will have. You will also start to come up with better answers to the questions the ball asks you on a regular basis.

Understanding What Is, Giving Credit

As a point or rally wraps up, a good question to ask is, "Was that a great shot by my opponent?" If so, then acknowledge that, and tell them, "good shot". This takes the pressure off of you and creates good conditions of sportsmanship in the match. Practicing gratitude and showing appreciation are key brain plasticity traits, and those also function to take the pressure off of you, when you acknowledge your opponent.

The Body Question

The next question to ask is "Was I in a good position, posture, and balance to hit the shot?" If not, then your opponent did something right. If you were, then you can stop and think for a moment, why did I miss?

Was I in a position to hit a good shot?
Why or Why not?

Those are the shots that you really want to make a very high percentage of the time. Understanding why you missed and looking for the most common misses can lead you to have a great lesson with your coach, to solve that problem moving forward.

The Internal Question

Another great question to ask is, "Did I choose the right shot?" If you are standing outside the alley and you went for a winner down the line, it's great if you make it, but it's a low percentage play, instead try a high deep crosscourt lob. If you chose the wrong shot, then tell yourself what you want to do the next time you are in that position. Pre-programming your mind can set you up to make better decisions moving forward.

Could I have attempted a higher percentage shot?

I have directly coached thousands of individual matches with players who come with a wide range of skills and experience. Many arrive in my programs with precious little competitive experience. Even the ones who played a lot of tournaments, still need a lot of training, in the mentality of how to play their match. They often don't understand that it's easier to reduce the number of errors in a match than it is to increase the number of winners. When you start going for too much, you may end up making many more mistakes.

Chapter Ten

How Do I Execute Technical Solutions?

Solving some technical issues, learning how to hit a certain kind of shot to play the ball a little bit better, fitting into a tactical situation, can boost your ability to play a certain strategy. If you want to come to the net, but you miss 20% of your approach shots, that puts a lot of pressure on you to win the remaining 80% of points. So take a lesson on approach shots, but make sure there is a live ball aspect to the training, then make sure you play some practice points and matches before you go live with that play. If your first serve percentage is below 60%, you are working too hard to win, because you have to hit a lot of extra serves, risk double faults, and defend your second serve. Learn a reliable spin serve for the first serve, from your local tennis pro, and you will not have to work as hard to win.

Spending one hour working on the one most common error you make, and reducing it by 25 to 50%, can be the difference in close matches.

When you think your way through a match, studying the

weakness of the player on the other side of the net, you can increase their errors, while reducing your own. You will do this by finding out which shots you hit, creating errors for them, or giving them opportunities to make their own mistakes. Working on your ability to hit the ball to targets allows you to execute this in live play. One of my players played a young guy who seemed to make a most ridiculous error on soft high bouncing balls in the middle of the court, blasting them in the net again and again. What should have been an amazing offensive opportunity for the opponent, became demoralizing errors. My player sent one or two of those shots per game because it was almost an automatic point.

> *You are the second most*
> *important player on the court.*
> *~ Craig O'Shannessy*

Take advantage of your opponent's weaknesses, and you will find your confidence growing. Also, spend time learning to work with certain patterns that work for you against most players, let that be an expression of your skills and personality. Over time you will begin to use more shot patterns intentionally, or somewhat accidentally, but learn to be opportunistic. You need to do both of those. Tennis Strategy 201 will build on this foundation you have begun.

First Technical Adjustments With A Caveat

No matter your personality, anxiety level, or style preferences, one thing technically you can do is shorten your backswing to make fewer errors. You can turn nervous energy into more precise footwork, moving into a better position to receive the ball. Once you get into a groove, catching the ball on your strings nicely, so you can send it up and over, then you can win. Once you have this confidence, you might reach back with a little big bigger backswing. However, if you are completely obsessed with the 'sending skills' of tennis, stroke technique, and the like, you might find that winning is a mystery because you are lacking a true fundamental to staying in a point. You can gain significant help to your game, if you put away some of the groupthink, the gaggle of conventional wisdom, the 'You Should Do This' off the 3.5 genius, reflecting on what actually works to win. Learn to filter your information, by not blindly accepting advice from just anyone, always filter it. Be open to real wisdom from anyone, because if it proves true, then the source doesn't matter. The echo chamber of most players and teachers will tell you that fixing technical issues, is the major factor in winning a match, when in reality, it has more to do with reading and reacting to the ball, thus getting into the ideal position for the ball strike.

Know the true fundamentals for staying in a point.
It usually does not have to do with how
good your strokes look.

Grow your interest in learning to receive the ball with great precision. Consider that most sports, featuring a ball, require you to gain possession of it, before you dribble, pass, throw or shoot. The positioning to gain control of the ball is essential. People often talk about how many of the top 100 players in the world grew up on clay courts, however maybe more importantly, they also played other sports like soccer (football), baseball, basketball, where they had to use their athleticism to accept the ball well, first.

So far, we have been discussing mainly ideas for shifting your mindset, now we will move toward the practical actions you can take to play better and win more.

I try to avoid teaching too much technique, because that has been covered by much better and more knowledgeable people than myself. I strongly recommend that you engage with Jack Broudy, who has been one of the top five most influential mentors in my teaching. Full disclosure: I am an affiliate with his website, and you can be as well.

Chapter Eleven

I Practice The Way Tennis Is Played?

To the man who only has a hammer,
every problem looks like a nail. ~ Mark Twain

Somewhere between 10,000 and 50,000 times in my career, I have seen a player who missed a shot, followed by that player, taking a practice swing to correct what they thought was a broken shot technique. The problem is that the stroke wasn't the problem, it was the footwork, but you don't see people practice footwork like that very often. The obsession with technique is the hammer, people less wise than you, see only the nails, in their swings at the ball. You will do well to check out my book Visual Training for Tennis, which will start you in the right direction as to a more logical starting place for learning how to hit the ball. Start with your eyes and your mind, they will guide your feet, and then to a simpler way to address the ball. The point is that often the root cause of missing a shot, is mostly something other than your technique, and if it were your technique it can be easily solved with shorter backswings as mentioned in the previous chapter.

The problem isn't the problem.
It's your attitude about the problem,
that's the problem!
~ Cap'n Jack Sparrow

Practice Footwork With Positioning

If you haven't moved well enough, to get in a good position for your shot, and you find yourself lunging, or too close, to the ball, then again you have created for yourself, an unforced error. Whether you were a bit slow, low intensity, or late to react, that can lead to errors. Some of you have the opposite problem of being overly anxious, overreacting, going too fast, and taking too many steps, which can also be a source of mistakes. While in general, more accurate footwork is a great idea, there can be a problem of too much of a good thing. A major issue I have with the conventional wisdom surrounding footwork is that people seem to think, "If some footwork is good, then more footwork is better.", but the reality is that you want exactly the right amount. It happens that a player will have a ball all lined up, take one or two extra steps, and work themselves out of position.

I'm going to use Precision Footwork.
Say this to yourself 5x before you start playing.

A lack of accurate footwork causes many issues. So, in my teaching I ask my players to use precision footwork, without even explaining how to do it, they often quickly figure it out themselves. How refreshing is that? While there is tremendous value to be found in learning 40-something contact moves for a shot, it's better to contain them in the phrase Precision Footwork. From there you may want to learn one particular move in which you are deficient, and build that into your game, until it becomes very precise. The one move I find my players taking some time to master is initiating their footwork by turning their knees and hips in the direction they want to move.   Be sure that you understand, the more you are thinking about your feet, the less you are thinking about the ball. In the short run, thinking about your feet will make shot-making more difficult.

Accurate Footwork

Precision Footwork doesn't make you think about your feet too much, but "Turn, shuffle, step, jab, recover, crossover, pivot, ready position", does make you think too much in the short term. When I can identify an issue with moving to a certain kind of ball, I will pay attention to that particular move, and practice only that one for a short while.

Practice footwork, receiving the ball with
short backswings, learning to move different ways
for shots that you have struggled to return.

You will have to be in a good position for your shots if you are going to send it where you want on the other side of the court.

Chapter Twelve

Why Do I Need A Coach?

People who have a coach improve 30-40% faster.

One of the most obtuse observations made by tennis pundits, on the boob tube, over the years is "Player X hits two big targets on the court". It's not very a precise analysis, as almost every player on tour, is capable of hitting very small targets on the court, regularly, at will. One drill Robert Lansdorp, who trained 5 different players to be #1 in the world, uses with his top players is to place a ball can, upside down, on top of a broom handle, threaded through the squares in the net, that is standing in the center of the court. Robert says that Maria Sharapova hit the ball can 8 times in a row. The better the player, the smaller the target on the court that players can hit.

Accepting shots that are in the neighborhood of the target area is a mental skill, while still attempting to hit very small targets.

If you are shooting for a bullseye on the tennis court, and you happen to miss by a foot or two, that target should be at least a few feet inside the court. Your targets should be set up so that if you miss a few feet in any direction your ball won't go out. Balls on lines and in corners are happy accidents. A separation between good and great players is that greater players can hit smaller targets, thus executing shot combinations with better precision.

When Not If... You Take Lessons

When you go for lessons with your coach, you want to train the accuracy of the shot, which allows you to create advantages in the geometry of the court. Essentially, it comes down to paying attention to the angle of your racquet face. We will cover in future chapters, how to take your newfound skill, of hitting targets on the court, to play certain strategies. The ability to hit targets on the court is similar to learning scales in music. It opens up your ability to improvise on the court. More importantly, you will be able to run set plays, to proactively win points, either by forcing errors or getting the occasional lucky winner. If you aren't yet aware of the data, regarding how tennis matches are played, consider that the SwingVision app, which I am an ambassador for, has reported from all matches input for 2021, that 74% of points end, before the fifth shot, has been successfully made. Do you want to start the point-hitting targets, or do you want to wait until after the 5th shot?

Interpreting The Data

This data includes all of those people who say their agenda is to be 'consistent'. The 0-4 tracking of point play, does not describe an intentional, breakneck, 'First Strike' obsession. Some coaches interpret the data to mean, that coaches who teach using these numbers, are advocating that you should end the point as quickly as possible. That's not true, but you don't mind if your opponent loses quickly. Do you want to play the first two shots more intelligently than your opponent? Of course, you do. If your opponent is only thinking about simply making the shots 'in', but you have an intention for where you want to place your serve and first shot or return and next shot, then you are playing more intelligently. When you consider that if you make your first two shots, you will have an advantage over the player that misses one of the first two shots, then hit to a safe target for each one keeps you in the point, but if you have targets for the shots, you take it up a notch and become more difficult to play.

In the next chapter, we will discuss a skill that will help you hit the ball more accurately.

Chapter Thirteen

How Does Spin Help Me?

Spin to win. ~ Tennis Maxim

Do you feel as though you struggle to place the ball where you want, and often hit the ball way out, left, right, or in the net, when you want to hit a spot? Spinning the ball could be a large part of the solution. After you make up your mind, that you want to mindfully learn to hit targets, the physical skill that supports that is using a manageable amount of spin. A word of caution is that some people are so obsessed with trying to hit 5,000 RPMs of spin, that they compromise their accuracy of the shot, with frequent mishits. So don't go crazy with spin.

Aerodynamics of Spin - Bernoulli's Principle

The tennis ball that is hit relatively flat, may waffle through the air a bit, like a knuckleball. It's been proven, that a spinning ball, can be delivered more accurately, like the spinning bullet from a rifle, compared to the inaccurate pellet from a musket. Because a spinning ball flies through the air in a more predictable path, this allows you to control it better. As the ball spins, pressure builds upon the part of the ball that is spinning forward, then like a rock skipping on a lake, it rides the air better, and tiny whirlpools of air surround the ball, like ball bearings, support a spinning shaft. The best thing is to learn one reliable spin, hit a certain way before diversifying your shots. We will dig much deeper into various spins in the next book, but now we will give a primer on the basic spins you need to understand as a newer player.

Topspin

This is the spin people use the most, and obsess about the most. People have topspin envy, but maybe they shouldn't. This kind of spin is a staple, very important to use, but used intelligently, it works way better than used without thought.

Benefits of Topspin

Ball in
Angles
Hit Hard
Change Of Pace
High Balls
Offensive Lobs
Passing Shots
Mitigates Friction With Ground

Liabilities of Topspin

Need Higher Incoming Ball
Need Faster Shot From Opponent
Easier to Mishit
Lands Short Often
Sits Up For Flat Shots

Muted By Under-spin/Slice
Need Good Timing
Requires The Most Effort

Benefits Of Slice

Easy to time
Easy to get deep
Can Sail Long
Easy To Vary
Might Skid Along The Court Surface
Requires The Least Effort
Great For Drop Shots
Great for Defensive Lobs
Great for Change of Pace
Great for Approach Shots
Stays Low

Liabilities of Slice

Flies Slow
Might Float
Can Be Overused
Not often offensive

Looks look at TopSpin V. Slice, then you can refer to the chart below for comparisons in regard to particular qualities of the ball flight, reaction to the court, and effect on the opponent.

More On Topspin

Topspin can help you learn to hit the ball a little harder

and keep it in the court. Because the ball lands a bit shorter, you can make shorter angle shots, pulling players off the court. If your spin is just right, even though the ball is not as fast as a flatter shot when it engages the court you can reduce the amount of friction, and the ball does not slow down as much when it hits the ground. You can use it to make the ball go higher against your opponent.

Slice Or Underspin

Slice shots have a much wider effect at the bounce, and on the final arrival to your opponent. Some slices can be offensively struck 'worm killers', while others are very slow flying, seem to come down for a landing and almost reverse themselves, giving the opponent less ball speed to work with to hit a power shot back. We will break down the wider variety of slice shots in Tennis Strategy 301.

The pace of a ball is an elusive term that seems to combine the speed of the shot with the weight delivered behind it. The ball compresses and stretches based on how it was hit, and some balls traveling the same speed, don't deliver the same weight of shot and explaining it is a bit elusive, but when you feel it, you will know it.

The serve presents some slight confusion because of the names of things, but it's not hard to reconcile.

Chapter Fourteen

How Does Spin Help My Serve?

*You can only try to make your serve in,
or you can aim for a specific place
in the service box for a specific purpose.*

Practicing your serve intelligently can help with your effectiveness in a match. First, take your time. When you play, 99% of the time you are going to have only two attempts. You don't hit serve after serve, and there is that time when you step up to the line to hit the first serve, practice that including your rituals.

Safe Effective Targets As You Get Started

When practicing serves, I always put the bullseye of my targets inside the service line by at least two feet. You can put them inside the sideline, or centerline by the same distance. When I teach beginners, I place a target about three full feet inside the service line. It is also placed right in the center of the box, students can miss by 6.5 feet wide, left or right, and still make the serve. Placing the target deep in the service box helps train players not to hit into the net. As you read earlier, this makes it necessary to accept that some serves will go long. In addition, there will be some balls that accidentally go perfectly in the corner, for an ace, and people will applaud, but that doesn't mean you will change your target in the short term. Simply accept some happy accidents and go back to aiming at your safe targets for ideal risk: reward. Every once in a while you might have a magical time when, playing in the zone, your shots will go on the line more often, and you are on, that's great, but you also have to have a conservative plan, for when that is not happening. On any particular day that you feel like you are struggling, come back to hit the ball deep center, especially on windy days.

After You Gain Control

After you start to gain some control of your serve placing it into the forehand and backhand, you can start intentionally moving your service around, in an attempt not to be too predictable. You can hit one side twice in a row but then alternate again. Be sure not to overthink it, because a predictable serve that is in, is much better than an unpredictable one that is out. Even if you determine that an opponent's backhand return is terrible, you still want to keep them honest by occasionally serving to their forehand. When practicing, simply use something to split the box in half, practice alternating shots in each box.

Once You Can Hit Three Targets

Consider also how your targets affect the other player. If you hit the ball away from them, they have to run. Hitting the ball at their body, makes them get out of the way of the ball. When you serve your first few serves, right at the opponent, you set the tone for them to protect themselves. If your service really did create a bit of a threat, they will hesitate a brief moment on future serves to the outside, because they will first feel like they will need to protect themselves. That slight hesitation will make it harder for them, to move to your serves, which are closer to corners.

Wide, Body, and T Serves

Mental /Emotional Effects Of Serve Targets

The way you target your shots can have a mental and emotional effect on your opponent. No one should get their feelings hurt if you hit the ball right at them, but sometimes people take it personally, even though it's part of the game. Your intent should be to win the match, and not necessarily to hit them with the ball. You definitely should check on their well-being if indeed they are hit, but it rarely happens. Anyone who has played any kind of physical sport will find that getting hit by a tennis ball, is no big deal. "Are you OK?", speak with real concern, which is more appropriate than saying, "Sorry", because, if you apologize, the assumption is that you won't try to do that again. So don't sign a social contract to never try to hit in their direction again, otherwise, you will compromise your game.

One way to be more confident that you won't hit someone in the face is to learn how to hit your targets better.

Chapter Fifteen

Why Can't I Hit My Targets?

As soon as the archer aims, the target moves.
~ Zen and The Art of Archery

Hitting targets with a ball delivered from the strings is largely a mental skill. People who have trained themselves in aiming projectiles will have a bit of an edge here, whether they were archers, shooters, played darts, or throw a ball at a target of any kind. Hitting to a target can invoke a kind of pressure that you won't feel if you hit aimlessly.

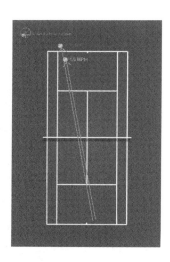

The ability to hit the ball where you want is a much higher priority than how fast you hit, how many spins you have, or how good your stroke looks. It doesn't matter how fast your service is if the ball goes out, and/or it puts you in a bad position to make the next shot. The way you play your shots can affect your ability to play a strategy. The more accurate your shots, the better able you are to run plays against your counterpart. Falling all over the place does not set you up well to play tactics that support strategies. The ability to hit shots and recover well goes hand in hand, because of the balance you need to do both.

Serve To Targets

When you're trying to improve your serve, practice hitting to a certain spot right. It's important to learn to hit targets. The first thing that happens when you bring out a target onto the court, is that players feel pressure. A coach might also feel pressure to help their player hit the target now! Feelings of pressure can create many different responses, most of them not very good. Rather than treat those symptoms, reduce the pressure.

Targets help players come to realize the internalized the pressure they feel to perform, even when no one asked them to feel that way.

When I get a target out, I ask my player how much power does this cone or circle has in your life? They say, none. But, then we proceed to try to hit the target, and the feelings inside them come and go. The problem seems to come from expectations of success. Hitting the target makes you a winner, missing the target is a failure, in the mind of the student.

Shift To Process Of Learning

The best practice of learning to hit targets is simply to pay attention to how it feels, and what it looks like when you swing. Take that experience, and pair it with the result of your shot, tell yourself, "When I swing like that, it goes there". Go through this process, of learning to hit closer and closer to targets. Also, you will need to learn to accept compensation, and over-compensation, because both are valuable. I don't know how many times I have seen a player hit the ball 10 feet too far, and 5 feet to the right, only to see the next serve, go nearly 10 feet short, and approximately 5 feet to the left. If the next shot goes somewhere between those last two shots, then learning to approximate has begun. Sometimes a player hits a ball nearly between the two and nearly hits the target. The experience of hitting the two previous shots, then the request to do something in the middle is the way forward. "Please give me a shot in the center of the last two shots".

When I swing like that,
The ball goes to that place.

The great thing about targets is that you can shift your mind, from subjective judgments of a good shot and a bad shot to an objective understanding, of how far the ball was from the target. You can learn to trust how your brain and body interact to make subtle adjustments in your swing and hand position to create the angle which helps you to learn to hit the target. The problem is trying too hard. As soon as you start trying too hard to aim your shot, the tension you create makes your muscles not flow as well. That's when the target seems to move. Simply attempt, to look how far from the target, ask yourself to hit the ball closer to the direction of the target, and make another attempt. Through experimentation, you will gradually learn the adjustments that give you the shot you want. All of this occurs outside of your higher-level thoughts. When you shift to thinking about how to do it, subjective judgments of the shot, building checklists, or telling yourself what to do as you do it, those things interfere with the simple process of hitting shots and objectively observing the result to allow your brain to learn what comes next. Those other ways, that many are predisposed to do, lead only to frustration. Frustration leads to trying too hard, stress and tension. Stress and tension lead to despair, and despair leads to quitting. Anyone reading this is welcome to a 20-minute consultation on this topic. I cover this topic in much more depth in Visual Training for Tennis.

Once you can hit targets, you will want to immediately start putting the new skill to good use, so that you can play intelligently from the beginning of the point until its end.

Chapter Sixteen

What Can I Learn From My Shots Results?

You can learn a lot from the outcomes of your shots. In fact, this is one of the most overlooked ideas behind how to learn to play tennis, and how to win a match under strange conditions. When you think about it. As we discuss elsewhere, when you start overthinking and judging your shots, when you start analyzing, how to do I that, or making a conscious decision when to swing, then you will be lost at sea. However, if you simply observe the outcomes of your shots, then you can start to understand what are the root causes of those shots. Then you can work on one aspect of your shot. Take a look at the diagram below on the following page. Out of the ten shots, four of them are wide and the others are in a bit of a high risk area except for one that we could call a safe target. This clearly shows that the racquet is meeting the ball at an angle out in front that does not allow for a safe target. It could be because of some impatience to hit the ball, and it many times is exactly that. It could be that this player is learning to make some angles, and will have to tolerate a few out wide until they perfect their timing. Simply observe your shot, then say, "If I hit that way, it goes to that spot in that arc."

Impatience?

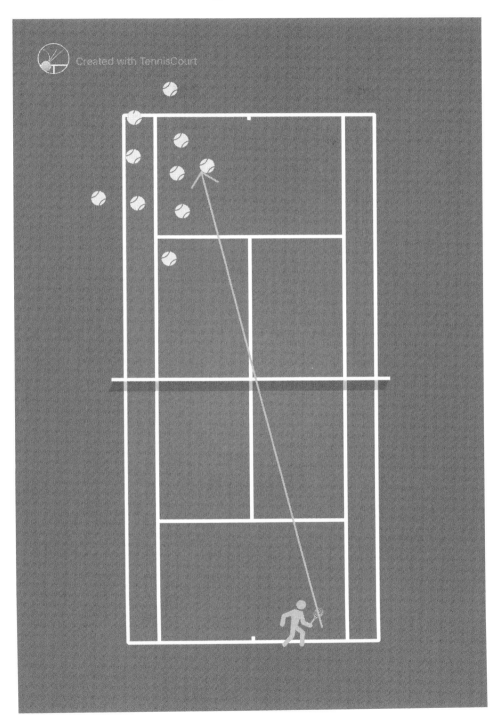

Take A Lesson To Establish A Contact Point.

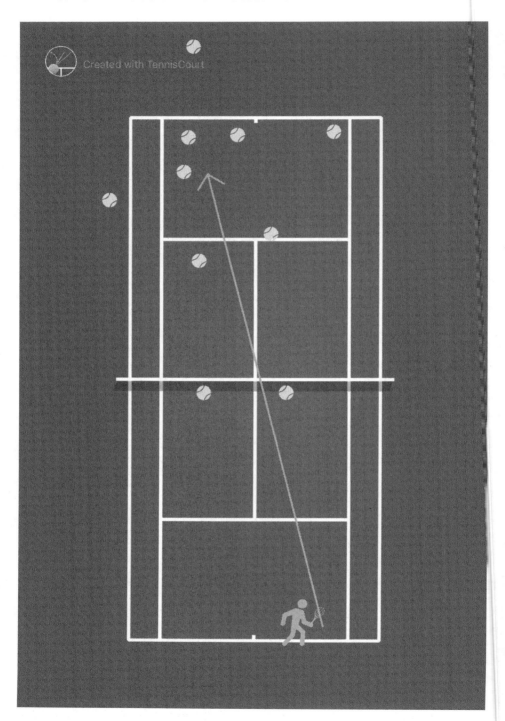

This Pattern Is OK For Basic Direction Of Balls, But You Are Overreacting To Deep Balls.

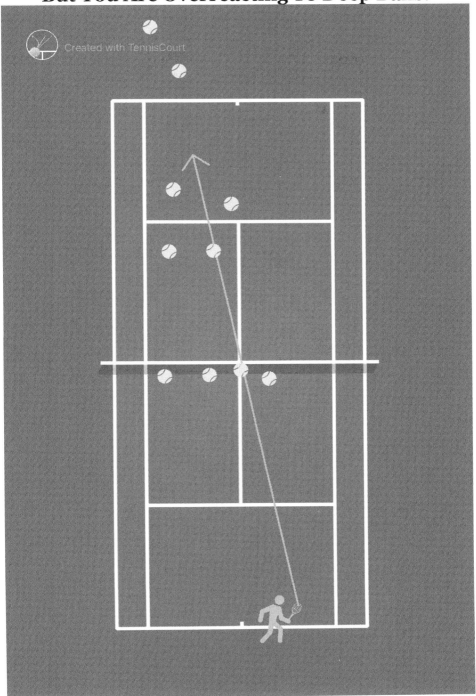

Improvement. But Hit Fewer Balls Too Long

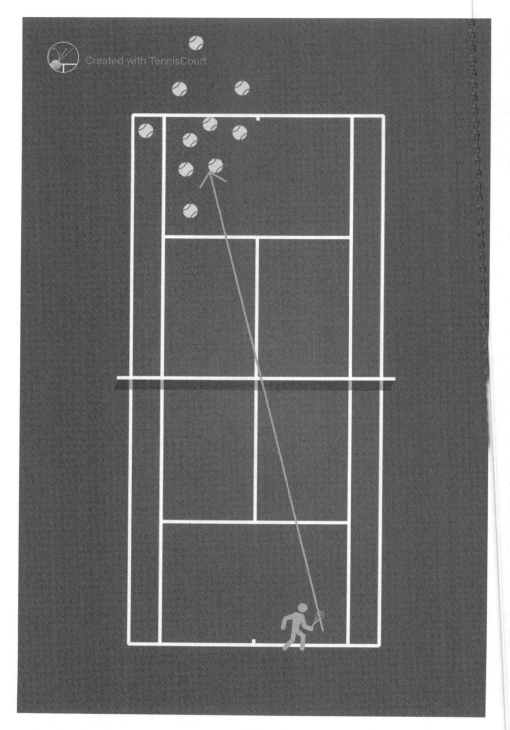

66

Chapter Seventeen

What Are Smart Targets?

In Congruent Tennis, we divide game development into 3 simple levels- 1,2,3, and use "Dual Objectives" to explain the supporting reasons. Here is an overview of the three levels, before we take a deeper dive into level one which is most appropriate for the level of play in this book.

Level 1 Tennis

Players show the ability to rally from behind the baseline. Players at this level might not have a fully developed spin game, but can make first and second serves, and understand how to play them differently. Learning to rally forehand and backhand shots with topspin and underpin will create an advantage against lesser players.

Level 2 Tennis

These players learn how to step inside the baseline, moving forward in the court to mount attacks against shorter, weaker balls. This level builds on improving the basic 2nd serve to be more aggressive to different targets of the service box. An improved level of control of shots will be necessary to achieve this level.

Level 3 Tennis

The most aggressive level of tennis is focused on point ending shots, closer to the net, along with aggressive serves that don't come back, and placing your opponent under much more pressure with your play. Players at this level take advantage of most every opportunity to finish with down the line shots, angled winner with ground strokes or volleys, and can finish a point with an overhead. These players will also be satisfied when their attempts for winning shots result in forced errors, which they many times will, knowing that they caused the error on the other side.

See The Future, But Start At The Beginning

It's an exciting time for you as the Level 1 player, because you are experiencing a lot of rapid improvement. Keep in mind as you go making improvements becomes a bit more difficult, but keep at it, and you will get where you are going.

Take on the challenge of learning the basics, before trying to move on to more advanced skills that that will pay off for you later. Buy into the process of improvement learning this framework. Each level is a prerequisite for future levels. Top players still use the first level thinking so that they can keep the ball going. They might be rallying at higher speeds, but they are still being careful at that higher level.

As you gain confidence in your ability to rally, then you will also be able to gain the ability to hit the ball harder. What goes into a good rally shot?

One of the most obvious markers of a basic rally shot is the net clearance height. Even top players normally hit their Rally shots 3-6' over the top of the net and you should too.

On average many top players shots are between 2 and 3 feet above the net, but when they are keeping the ball going, they hit a bit higher.

Cooperative Rallies For Skill Development

Hitting several feet above the net satisfies the Dual Objectives. You want your ball to be much less likely to go into the net, and to give better length for your shots, into the opponent's court. Most coaches call this a deep shot. While having good length to your shots is important, it isn't helpful as helpful if you get carried away with hitting so deeply, as a new player. Using a more moderate length for your shots, makes it less likely your shot will miss long, also your partner will have an easier time returning your ball, for better practice. When you provide this courtesy, to each other with your shots, it facilitates more of a cooperative rally. You then will get more hits in, and find that you won't have to retrieve the ball as frequently. It is also much more enjoyable to move to continuously hit shots, getting a better workout. Now that you have a basis for practice, you are ready to think about the targets.

What Are Smart Targets?

Knowing and understanding Smart Targets is one of the most important things a player needs to grasp in this concept of strategy. Inexperienced players often choose poor targets, because they are considering the geometry of the court without thinking about the other player. Aiming closer and closer to the lines, adjusting the target wider, due to the movement of the opponent. In the heat of the moment, players see the opponent moving to the left where they are about to hit, then adjust their shot more to the left overreacting to the opponent's movement. While that is an intuitive thing to do, it often leads to going too far left, with the ball, missing wide. When you know your smart targets, you hit to them based on the opponent's position, but they anchor you, so that you don't overreact.

Understanding The Lanes

A key aspect of smart targets, is understanding that they exist within lanes on the court. When coaches put cones out on the court, they commonly suggest a place for the ball to bounce, rather than a zone to hit into, so adjust your targets, so that they encourage you to hit through these areas. We call the path the ball follows The Line of Shot. You can gain an advantage when you successfully place a ball through the better hitting lanes. Your shot should have an intention behind it, as has been mentioned already in this book. You can learn to recognize the different kinds of lanes to hit into, now look at the diagram below. You can see that the hitting lanes are a few feet inside the court on the sides, and 3 full feet from the baseline in the longest corner of the smart zone triangle. Do you see where the court is marked as 39' from the net to baseline? Now look to the marking of 36' to the end of the smart target area.

Smart Target And The Avoid Zone

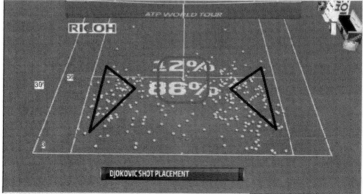

DJOKOVIC SHOT PLACEMENT

Smart Targets are black rectangles that are inside the court by two or three feet. The Avoid Zone is directly in the center of the court, which leaves your ball open to attack.
The Avoid Zone

The red section in the center of your opponent's side of the court is the Avoid Zone. Hitting to the smart targets will help you stay away from this zone, where you would be giving your opponent a forehand in the center of the court. However, as stated earlier, this is a good zone to hit into when you are simply keeping the ball going with a friend to develop your rally skills. One best practice is to set a number of 10 shot rallies you will have before you start trying for smart target shots. Make sure you and your partner are warmed up and making many shots before going to the wider lanes on court. You can also practice having one player hit into the avoid zone, and the other player hitting to smart target, taking turns in each role. Balls that land in the Avoid Zone, give the most options for attack to the opponent.

Moving The Ball To The Sides Of The Court

So, early on for a confidence boost, warm up down the middle with easy shots, then as you get warmed up, move the ball closer to the sides of the court, while still keeping them safely in by a few feet. It is important to remember this will not be a good hitting lane for matches, so don't train yourself to hit short in the middle, as it should only be used for confidence building and warm up. Players who practice too much up the middle, find it difficult to hit the ball away from their opponent. How you practice the most will take over in your subconscious and you will play that way in a match.

Djokovic Ball Placement, Very Few In The Middle

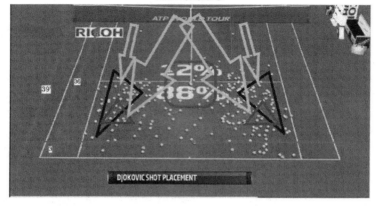

Note the percentage of balls that land in the service boxes, and how the vast majority of his shots land in the smart target area or nearby, very few balls land near the lines.

Developing The Lanes For Change Of Direction

Once you have developed your cooperative rally skills, you can build on that, by using the down the line hitting lane, for keeping the ball going straight ahead. See the small yellow arrows in the Djokovic Diagram. Next, stand diagonally from each other, to hit crosscourt, as noted by the light blue arrow below. The green X's below show where you stand to hit with a crosscourt cooperative rally.

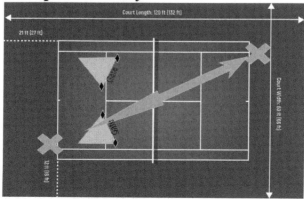

Crosscourt shots also keep you from hitting into The Avoid

Zone.

You can set some cones or court markers on the court in the position of the black diamonds to practice hitting through the gates. As shown in the diagram, these are fairly wide gates, but will be challenging to the newer player to gain control over the shot to hit through those lanes, but when you begin to master it, you can control the court.

What The Future Holds

When you go for the black diamond that is placed more to the center of the court, that is a more conservative play. Conversely, when you go for the outside black diamond there is a bit more risk involved in that play, even thought the target is fully two feet inside the court.

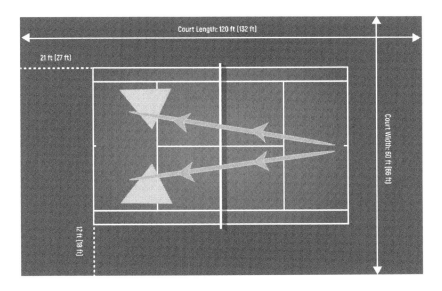

Chapter Eighteen

What Is First Strike Tennis?

We remember the longer rallies because they are more exciting.

In the battle of perception and reality, perceptions always win. How can we align our perception better with what is really happening in matches? The first thing we need to realize is that we have better memory for the exciting things, and less space dedicated to the dull occurrences in a match. People still rave about the 27 shot rally on match point, where the champion succeeded. Very thrilling. But, they forgot the serves that went unreturned, and they forgot every time the server failed to hit their second shot. Those are not salient, because frankly, they are disappointing. As a fan, that's not what you want to see.

As a player, you are more likely to remember the rallies that are 9 shots and more, the exhilaration, fear, the emotional and physical investment in playing them. When you play a long point, it feels like it's worth more, but in reality, it's not. When you lost a 57 shot rally point, followed by your opponent double-faulting, it's 15-all. So, instead of wishing for every point to be nine shots or more, which will leave you exhausted, learn to play the percentages of what really happens. I teach my players that same thing and then they don't obsess so much on having won or lost a long point. The effort you put into a point does not increase its value. Pay attention to how short many points really are.

The Short Points Are Major

We shift our attention to winning the type of points that occur the most because we want to major in the majors. The conventional wisdom of rallying and consistency prepares you for the points that happen way 10-25% of the time.

Plan Two Shots At A Time, Maybe Three

First Strike tennis is an important concept to understand, you want to know how to do it effectively. First Strike tennis might be a bit of a misnomer because it could be called First Plan Tennis, the point being that the player who has a plan for the earliest shots, in a point, has an edge over the one, who does not. That plan does not include, losing the point immediately. So, for those of you who are assuming, that I mean someone should recklessly go for aces and winners on the first two shots, you have another thing coming. You will make things much more difficult for yourself if you go for reckless offense in the first two shots. Losing points needlessly and early will make the match much harder to win.

First Strike - Playing the first two shots with a game plan.

No Strike - Playing scared to miss, never making anything happen, only responding to opponent's plan.

Someday Strike - Wait until you hit x number of shots before you try to do something smart. X may never come.

*Death Flower Strike - Go for winners on every shot, regardless of errors made.

Using Data To Play Smart

In the last 10 years the data in regard to how tennis matches are actually played and won has entered into the mainstream, not without some controversy. This data has had to go through the stages of truth. There are still many who ridicule the data, because they are so deeply attached to the word 'consistency', that they have a hard time accepting the fact, that most points end before you have a chance to make a third shot.   Some players and coaches, wrongly assume, that training according to the reality of rally lengths, means trying to end the point immediately. They are wrong.

Most Points Are Short, Period

It bears repeating, Swing Vision shared: 74% of all points ended before the 5th shot is made. On the pro tours, men's matches finish 70% points before the 5th shot, and women's 65% end before that threshold is reached. Styrling Strother took over 40,000 data points and found that these stats hold up at the high school level of play.

Should you try to end a point quickly?
Yes and No. Yes if you are winning most
of them, and no if you are losing them most.

Anyone claiming that any of the data is cooked, or anecdotal has no standing. College coaches often scoff at this data, and show with pride, that the players they coach, play matches where in some matches, 55% of the points end under 5 shots. What they don't seem to realize is that it means that the majority of points end quickly. It's a head-scratcher. I would suggest that because they so strongly urge their players to grind early in points, they are not teaching them to take advantage of shot combinations from the beginning of the point, and thus are doomed to work too hard for their points. This also will not serve them well when they attempt to play professional tennis, where the vast majority of players have a game plan that includes smart point construction from the first shot.

Plan To Make The First Two Shots

Now that we hammered that, what do you do with that data? Short answer: make your first two shots, and you will win a lot of points, assuming the other player won't. Better answer: play your first two shots with targets in mind and you gain an additional advantage over a player who does not have that level of intentionality.

Chapter Nineteen

The Most Important Shot In Tennis?

Tennis Maxim 1: The Serve Is The Most Important Shot In Tennis

The serve is vital in tennis, because it starts every point, and the most common rally length is 1 shot. Make your serve, and your opponent will miss some returns. Miss your first serve, and your opponent will not miss your serve as often. They will miss 20% to 50% of them. If they miss 50%, you are probably having a boring match.

As You Improve Serve Placement Varies

Placing your serve into a certain part of the service box to then set up an initial combination of shots is something we are going to cover in a future chapter and also in greater detail in Tennis Strategy 201 and 301

First Serve Percentage = Win

Making your first serve almost certainly will give you a

higher winning percentage of points, compared to missing it, making your second serve or possibly double-faulting First serve percentage is the most important statistic in tennis, as pro men win slightly less than 3/4 of all points when they make their first serve. WTA women conquer 2/3 of all the points when the first serve goes in the box. The difference in that one statistic sheds light on why women have their serves broken more often, because of the relative lack of offensive power on the first serve, combined with a more empowered approach to the return game among women.

Second Serve = Danger

When you look at second serve stats, when compared to first serve results, in which over the course of a year, not one professional player wins more than 50% of the points. Winning second serve points comes with a cost of higher effort and a more defensive mindset. The serve is also among the most physically taxing shots. When you have to hit two of them, that's twice as much effort. If you miss three straight first serves, you have to make six serves instead of only three. There is an energy cost when you more frequently have to hit two serves instead of one. Consider a long match with 100 points played on your serve. If your serve percentage is 40%, then you made 40 first serves. Out of the hundreds of points, you will have played 60 missed first serves, and 60 second serve attempts, which will increase your double faults, for a grand total of 160 serves.

If you make your first serve,
you won't ever double fault.

However, when you make 60% of your serves, then you get 60 first serves, 40 missed first serves, and 40 second serve attempts. When you attempt fewer second serves, you will also double fault less frequently. Making first serves increases your confidence in making serves in general. The result of serving 60% of your first serves results in attempting 140 serves, and the energy savings of 20 serves can be the deciding factor in a close match on a hot day, especially combined with the corresponding winning percentages. Every once in a while someone will win more than 50% of second serve points, but its certainly not a benefit compared to the first serve win percentage. The more difficult the opponent, the more likely they can attack second serves effectively. The first part of the first strike is making your first serve.

Spin To Win

It's never too early to learn a spin serve, and a nice slice or sidespin serve is relatively easy to learn and control. Avoid trying for hard flat serves all the time, as this will diminish your first serve percentage, meaning that you will have to play more second serve points, which in turn will make it harder to win. We will get more into spin in a later chapter. Also, intentionally move your serve around in the service box, don't always hit the ball in the same direction. It's also wise to attempt to serve more often to your opponent's backhand, than to their forehand.

Chapter Twenty

What Is The Second Most Important Shot?

Tennis Maxim 2: The Return Of Serve Is The Second Most Important Shot in Tennis

If you can't return well, you will have to win all of your matches in tiebreakers, and hope to string a few returns together, at exactly the right time.   You will also have tremendous pressure on you, to hold your serve every time. The safest return, to assure the best possible percentage made is back to the server. When you practice with a friend, be sure to get some serve and return practice in as well. Since the second most common rally length is 2 shots, it's imperative that you make the return, otherwise, you lose the point quickly. Go for the safest possible shot, which allows your opponent to miss. When you miss your return, they don't get that chance to miss their shot.

Give the other guy a chance to choke.
~ Jimmy Connors

Newer, or lower-level players sometimes can live in a

fantasy world, where they see some of the top returners in the world, who just happen to have a ball go into their wheelhouse, striking a wow shot, amazing everyone and they want to do like their hero! But the fantasy player, who has been watching too many movies produced with CGI, engaging in hero worship, believes this is something they can try to do often. Actually, the opposite is true. The reality is that that serve that was crushed, was a mistake by the server, to allow that delivery to go right in the maw of the forehand strike zone, in the first place. You, not yet one of the very best returners in the game, should play the return of serve, simply to get it back into the court. If you can do that 75 - 80% of the time, that's amazing will force the server to make one more shot, more often than they want. When you hit it back in the same direction the ball came from, you are less likely to miss. When you don't change the direction of the shot, the timing is easier. Require the server to make a second shot to win the point! Remember the 2nd most common rally length is two shots, meaning that if you make the return, they will often miss their next shot.

Practice Return Of Serve

Sadly, people don't practice return of serve as much as they should, but this gives you an opportunity to gain an edge when you find a like-minded individual, who is willing the practice the secret sauce. Additionally, it's much better to practice for the server. Delivering the ball in for someone who is practicing their returns, brings a different kind of pressure that is stronger than match play. You feel an obligation to make the serve, for the sake of being a good practice partner. Pro Tip: Returners should try to return everything, even the balls that are out, because those balls are more challenging than normal serves and if you can make those, then serves in the box seem easier. Servers should be sure never to serve into the net, because the returner doesn't get to hit anything, but those balls that are a few feet long are still returnable. If you are competitive, find a friend who doesn't mind spending 10-20 minutes practicing serves and returns. It will do you a world of good.

Now we will discuss the difference in philosophy between returning first and second serves.

Chapter Twenty One

Do I Return All Serves The Same Way?

Returning first serves is almost always defensive, while addressing second serves can be an opportunity for offense.

Returning first serve generally means you will be facing the most defensive situation that occurs regularly. Big shots and netplay can be more offensive, but they don't occur as often. Treat returning the first serve carefully, and it's important to consider that even the greatest returners of serve make about 80% of them in the court. That means they miss one in five, and that includes second serve returns which improve the percentage. Great returners make 75-80% of their returns in play overall, so that means a bit less on first serves, and more on second serves.

How To Make More Returns

The safest thing to do is to use a very short backswing, use the power of the service against itself, and return the ball to the same direction from which it came. Changing the direction of the shot requires better timing and includes more risk. Simplify the way you put your strings on the ball, meet it head-on because going for a big topspin shot is more likely to produce a mishit. This will give you a huge edge and is the first part of making your first two shots. There are rare instances where your opponent has a very weak serve. In that case, you might be able to treat it like a second serve.

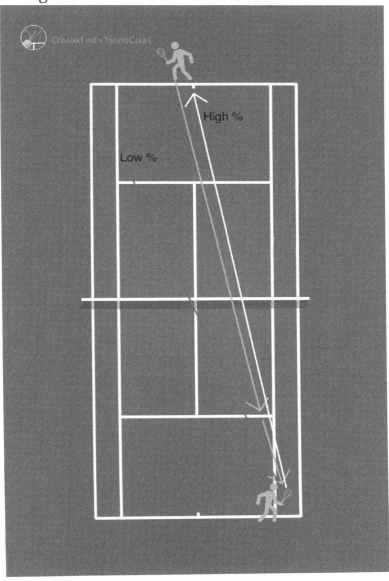

Returning Second Serve

Let's flip the data around, and consider 100 - x. On average, winning second serve points is around 45%, then that means you can expect to take advantage of a 55%, or more, win percentage when you attack someone's second serve. With a controlled aggression approach, to attacking second serves, you also ramp up the pressure, on your opponent. If you put them under enough pressure, they may also start to throw in some double faults.

Controlled Aggression For Second Serve

On hard courts, how well you attack second serve is one of the largest factors in winning the match. While you might tolerate a few more errors, if you are letting people off the hook by missing more than 1 in 10 second serves, then that's a good place to clean up what you are doing. Any more than 2 errors per 10 returns is not controlled aggression. Depending on how good the server is, the second serve might give you a tremendous opportunity, or just a slight crack in their armor. It has been said that you are only as good as your second serve, so as you go up the levels, it gets more and more difficult to attack the second delivery, but you should start now!

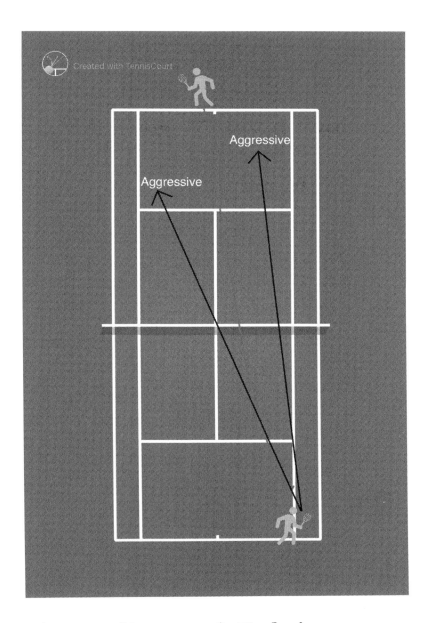

Facing An Idiosyncratic Technique

Try not to get too frustrated early on, if they have some idiosyncrasy in their second serve, making it difficult, for you to, time at first. In any event, unless you are making a lot of errors, you want to try for a hurt shot. Use the best tactic, that lines up with your strategy, whether it's a short angle return, deep crosscourt, a down-the-line approach shot, or forcing shot attempt or a drop shot. You want to test out how aggressive you can be and still make the shot. So, hit back at the server a little harder, make an angle cross-court, return down the line and come to the net, with a surprise drop shot, or lob. All of those things can help you take control of the point immediately. But finally, 'Controlled Aggression' means that you are making your shots with some margin to avoid an error.

Chapter Twenty Two

What About The Next Shot?

In the logic that is not connected to the data, people consider which are the most important shots to be the ones that are most impressive. They will say that forehands are important (and that's where there are so many Federer Forehand videos on YouTube), or backhands are more important, while a much more accurate way to think about winning your match is the 3rd and the 4th shots of a point. You have to make them in the court, or you lose, so the first objective is to be ready for those times when your opponent hits a great shot. Mentally, you want to expect your opponent to have some hard returns and great placements.

Defense First

Realizing that defending against attack is the highest early priority can save you a handful of needlessly lost points. Expect good shots from your opponents, and do not be surprised, so that you can better respond to the next ball. In the case that the other player is not attacking with their first shot, being able to shift quickly, to see if you will be taking advantage of a poorly struck ball is the next priority. The question is "where is it going?"

Contingencies Are Tennis

There are three contingencies that you must prepare for after you serve or return. 1. Play a defensive shot, because you are under attack. 2. Play a controlled aggressive shot, because you were given an opportunity. 3. Rally a ball deep crosscourt to reset the 'Control, Hurt, Finish' protocol. The first priority is to not lose, the second priority is to take advantage, and finally to reset playing a shot that combines offense with defense when the other two things don't happen.

You Have To Be Ready To Defend Any Of These Shots On Accident, Or Purpose

React, Don't Overreact

Not being surprised is not obvious, and so is the idea of

taking advantage of opportunities, and the main reasons are that players obsess about consistency. The player who is trying to make more shots where they want is also more likely to seize more opportunities because they recognize them. In a match where one player is taking advantage, and the other player is just wanting to make the shot, the second one fails to take advantage, surrendering leverage to win the point. This is one of the subtle differences between players, the proactive ones are better than the passive, or reactive players.

Take Advantage

Better players take better advantage of opportunities, to move forward on shots and play something with a little more power, a little more angle, or taking a little more time away, from the opponent. Your default shot could be a deep crosscourt because it combines defense and offense. But, part of the fun of tennis, is the improvisation that happens, when you get to come forward on a shot. You will start to discover, which kind of shots work well for you when you are playing with your feet way inside the court. The player with an agenda can beat the player without one.

When The Opponent Hits Here,
You Gain An Advantage...

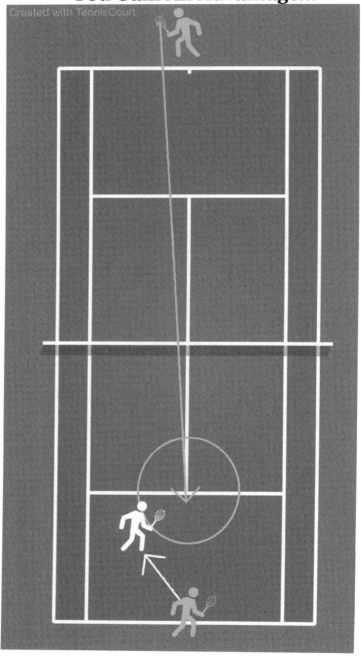

...If You Can Hit To Any Of These Places

Pre-Program Yourself For Defense First,
But Shift Quickly Into Controlled Aggression

Whether you have served or returned, there are a few objectives that you need to achieve. You want to be ready for the next shot. Seeing clearly to the other side of the court, and relatively still, but springy, so you can explode to the netball:

1. Recover to a balanced position as quickly as possible. If your strokes don't throw you off balance in the first place, it's easier to recover.

2. Shift your vision to your opponent's frame, while at the same time recovering, to bisect the angle of your opponent's possible returns. Split the area, into which, the other player can possibly hit their next shot.

3. If you are not able to get perfectly in the middle of the opponent's possible shots, when the ball has bounced, on their side of the court, then break down into the ready position, after one more step, right where you are. This can make it more difficult for them to 'wrong foot' you, hitting the ball behind you. When you have done it wrong, you will know what I mean and start to get into the ready position earlier.

4. Have a 'still' moment, where you are not moving in any direction just before your opponent strikes the ball so that you can be as ideally balanced as possible.

5. Take note of tendencies your opponent has on certain shots, from particular locations in the court. Look for a pattern on anyone common type of shot, like the one you are about to return, and look for the most likely shot first. This can help you to respond more quickly, to what they do most

often.

6. No matter what is coming, be open-minded to read and react to the ball coming out of their strings. Turning your knees and hips toward where you are going to run helps a lot.

Next, we will break down the philosophy for how to modify your game in one of the best technical solutions to tactical problems, along with five different factors.

The next chapter contains some great material, for the better players, in the target ability range of this book, and will help you gain better situational awareness, of how to alter your technique based on, where you are in the court. Technical solutions to tactical problems!

Chapter Twenty Three

Is There One True Stroke?

Do you know the pain of running up on a short ball, thinking that you are about to win the point, only to blast it long or wide? This chapter solves that problem. Then you won't have to say to yourself 'Not Again!!!'. When you understand how to play the ball differently in certain situations, you can reduce the number of dumb mistakes you make, just as I had to learn.

Attribution Of This System

It must be noted that I was first taught this system by Brett Hobden, a great Australian coach, but there has been some controversy over who developed it, promoted it, and/or owns it. If indeed it turns out to be trademarked, I will have to adapt this chapter in the future. I know there has been a dispute between different national governing bodies and major teaching organizations over its use and proper attribution.

Don't Overdo It

This is another concept that will dramatically help the 2.0-3.5 player, as I get so many players in a first lesson, who are over-swinging, or were never taught that you can vary your swings based on the situation. The kind of shot you receive from the other player, how fast you have to run, or whether you need to get out of the way of the ball have a bearing on your swing size and shape. By way of analogy, if you know how dense your forest is, then you will know which size machete to yield.

Five Factors That Affect Your Swing Size

Here is the Tennis Strategy 101 Tennis Map, but you will notice that it changes in 201, and again it morphs into different shapes for more advanced players. The reason being is that as you play, you start to understand the human factors of the geometry of the court more accurately, and with more nuance. Newer players tend to obey the rectangles and vertical lines, a bit much. As you improve you will start to understand the diagonals, and curves better, but all good things in time. Slow and steady wins the race. There are five factors that have a bearing on how you play your shot. There are two major factors and three minor factors.

The Major Factors

1. Where Are You In The Court?
2. How Big Is Your Backswing?

The Five Zones

There are five basic zones for the beginner, take a look at zone 4, you will spend the most time in that zone. You serve and receive from there, and you will rally often from the baseline, which means, even when both feet are just inside the baseline, you are still in zone 4. Once you are inside the court by at least three feet, you are then headed into zone 3.

If you learn nothing else, know this one thing,
the closer you are to the net, the smaller your
the backswing will be on every shot.

Baseline Deep

Once you are 5 feet or more behind the baseline, then you are in zone 5. If you go all the way to the back fence or wall, you now are minimum of 15' from the baseline, but you could be 30' or more. Most courts have a fence that is about 25' from the baseline. The court is 78' long, so when you add 25 feet, you are now 103' from the other baseline, which means you are at serious risk of hitting the next ball short, and if you do lay the ball up in front of your opponent, they have an opportunity to hit a very tough shot, if they go for a drop shot or an angle.

Mid-court Transition Zones

As you move forward into the court, take account of the fact, there is less court into which, you can keep your ball in play. That's why players often blast balls out long or wide when they come forward because they didn't account for the shorter distance. When you get into zone 3, you have 73' or all the way down to 60' to hit into. The service line is 21' from the net, and the other half of the court is 39'. That's why you need shorter backswings, because of the significantly shortened space, to accept your shot.

Greatest Variety Of Skills Required

Zone 2 and Zone 3 require the most decision-making and variety of skills. In either zone, you might have to volley, hit an overhead, want to hit a drop shot, half-volley, or either groundstroke, so the onus is on you to read and react to what is coming quickly. In 201 we will cover the decision-making necessary in those zones in greater depth. For now, realize that you will decide quickly what to play, stick with your decision, and take shorter backswings.

Avoid Overplaying In A Zone

From Zone 3, you decide quickly if you are attacking or retreating, but you must do one or the other. The big rectangle at the back of the court used to be called No Man's Land, but you know, what about women? I once heard it called The Rectangle of Death, which I like because it's not too dramatic. Anyway, in singles, you don't want to get stuck there, as it becomes very easy to beat you with angles in any direction. (In doubles, things change, because you have a partner, and transitioning to the net is so important). So from zone 3, you are either going forward to attack at the net, or you are hitting a defensive shot so that you can retreat to the baseline.   In zone 2 and 1, you won't hit a lot of groundstrokes, but you will hit a lot of volleys, overheads, a few half volleys, and drop shots or drop volleys. All of those shots require less swinging.

Pairing Backswings

Now, the second major factor pairs with the zones, like a traditional breakfast that you know so well, it's routine.

Breakfast is simple and routine for most people because you want to start the day right. Using the best fitting backswing length for the zone you are in the court is no different. The exceptions to the general rules are the minor factors, but we will discuss those a little bit later. Start with the racquet at the contact point approximately 45 degrees ahead of you. If you want some of the very best instruction on technique, check out Jack Broudy, one of the most influential mentors in my tennis

Ideal Contact Point

When I learned from Jack that the ideal contact points are approximately 45 degrees in front, it revolutionized my own game and solved a lot of mysteries for me and my players moving forward. With the string bed that is tilting ever so slightly back to lift the ball up over the net, making contact at that ideal place helps you make many more shots and become more efficient in doing so. Your frame is almost parallel to the net, depending on the angle you are hitting, I saw almost because it's not something about which you should obsess.

Contact Point Is The Origin

Now that you understand that contact is at 45 degrees, in front of you, or slightly behind that, (some people may end up with arm issues if they are too rigid about it), when the ball is in your frame, that is the origin, that is 0 on our curved number line. 0 backswing is where ball and racquet meet, 1 is the smallest backswing you can think of, 2 is 45 degrees back from 0. If we backtrack, a 1 sized backswing can be half or less of what 2 sized takeback is, so that would be 22.5 degrees or less, but try not to obsess about the exact angles. A 3 sized backswing points directly at the back fence, 90 degrees behind you, in its furthest backward movement, for many male pros, this is as far as they go. The racquet is 90 degrees away from and behind the contact point. A 4 sized backswing goes, 45 more degrees beyond the 3 size backswing, so don't break your brain over it being 135 degrees, away from the contact. For a 5, I call that anything bigger than a 4, and it's rarely used, as you will reach back for your maximum amount of swing, mostly on higher deeper shots in zone 5.

Start With 4

So, when you are serving, returning, and rallying from the baseline, in general, you are going to use 4 backswings. Many people overswing. Take a lesson with a pro, or film yourself to measure your backswings. If you find yourself over-hitting, or your timing is poor, you can use a 3 backswing in zone 4, until you gain confidence, then you can reach back for a little more.

Taking too short a swing is much better then taking too big a swing in any zone.

Chapter Twenty Four

What Are The Three Minor Factors?

Even a blind squirrel finds a nut now that then, and the seemingly non-offensive player can suddenly have a ball grooved perfectly to their forehand and meet it exactly right for a missile in your direction. You can hit that back with a shorter backswing. The more challenging the speed, the shorter the backswing. You might even use a 1 backswing in zone 4 as Federer often does, or a 2 backswing in zone 5 when returning a hard hit overhead.

How High Is The Ball

The higher the ball, the larger a cut you might need to take, and the lower the smaller, except that you won't often want a 1 backswing unless you are very close to the net. When you are pushed way back behind the baseline by 10 feet or more, that's time for a 5 backswing, on those high bouncing balls.

How Much Do You Have to Move For the Ball

In general, the faster you are moving with your legs the

slower and smaller you want to be moving with your hands. When you are on a maximum sprint to a ball, you will also generate the most energy onto the ball. Sometimes players are surprised and disappointed that they ran so fast to a ball, take a bigger swing because they think they should, only to blast the ball away of the court, or even over the fence. Hitting balls over the fence happens to everyone, but far less with higher-level players. As a new player, you might feel embarrassed to do it one time, but that will increase by a lot if you do it more than once. The key is to go slower and smaller with your swing.

You can see that the three minor factors create exceptions to the general rules of combining the top two factors of your location in the court and how that gives a starting point for understanding how big your backswing should be.

Chapter Twenty Five

Faster Shots Win Matches, Right?

80% of matches are won by the player who hits the ball more slowly.

It's only natural to assume that hitting the ball faster on average would lead to more wins, but it's not true. This runs counter to what people intuitively believe. Those of you who have been playing a while, understand the ability of pushers, slicers, and dicers, to win matches. Even in a highly competitive match between people who can sometimes hit 100 MPH forehands, the player who hits more slowly wins more often. The most simple reason is that the faster shots, often go out long or wide. Consider that a ball that was hit at 60 MPH was a foot out, if that same shot were hit at 55 MPH, it may have landed in the court.

Use Different Speeds On Purpose

Slower shots indicate a wider variety of skills. Players who hit faster are generally hitting with less spin, not often lobbing, hitting drop shots, or slicing the ball. Players who hit fast all the time, why do they do that? Is it because winners are salient, thrilling, and memorable? There is no mistaking the elation, the dopamine fixes you get from hitting a winner, but Vic Braden used to say, "That same boring winner", meaning winning the point intelligently, not with brute force. The boring winning shots are the ones that go in the court where we want them to go.

Benefits Of Slower Shots, They:

* land in the court sooner.
* don't travel as far.
* can be a drop shot
* buy you time to recover to bisect the angle...
* change the pace of the rally
* challenge the timing of your opponent
* take away power from the rally
* don't give your opponent free power
* give more time/space than your opponent wants

Risks of Slower Shots:

* they can go in the net
* they can land short in the court
* they can be an easy shot for your opponent
* hit into the center of the court they are attackable

Benefits of Faster Shots

* take away time and space from the opponent
* more likely to force errors
* more likely to be a winner

Risks of Faster Shots

* MORE LIKELY TO GO OUT LONG OR WIDE
* give your more powerful opponent pace
* give the slicer and dicer the pace they need

So, now you are wondering,
if I am getting pummeled by a strong opponent,
what can I do?

Chapter Twenty Six

What Is Shot Tolerance?

Developing shot tolerance is one of the best ways to find satisfaction in your tennis, because you will always be a tough out.

One of the most demoralizing feelings on a tennis court is that of feeling playing against a Howitzer Cannon. You are getting blasted, and just can't get those balls back, then you face the prospect of that happening again and again. It makes for a tough day at the office. Developing shot tolerance is a large part of the answer. We have already set the stage for shot tolerance, by examining the 5 factors for success, but now we are going to drill down into the shot tolerance aspect of it. As we started this work, people were obsessed about what they are going to try to do to their opponent, but then they are not prepared as well for what the opponent is doing to them. Flip that around, and make your main focus muting your opponent's offense, or taking advantage of their lack of it.

Be A Wall

If you can't resist the stronger shots of your opponent,

you are in danger of being overpowered. If you are thrown off by the player who makes you run or changes the pace, and you can't tolerate the movement or the difference in timing, then you are also at risk of being victimized. Yesterday I was working with a 3.0 player who has all the tools to be a 4.5 someday, but he is in a league with the slicers and dicers, the guys whose tennis games are like Ginsu Knives that you used to see on TV, so sharp they can cut paper. You get done playing them and you feel like you went through a food processor.

Play Further Back In The Court

The ball slows down considerably after the bounce. The closer you are to the bounce, the more pressure you will feel from its speed, and the further back the less. Of course, you don't want to let the ball bounce twice or play it off of your shoe tops very often, but you can find a happy medium. A number of years back John Yandell did a study that showed a Pete Sampras serve at approximately 120 MPH, would slow down to 85 MPH before it even bounced, because of gravity and air pressure. Once the ball hit the ground it would be around 65 MPH, then when it got to Agassi it was traveling only around 50 MPH. Agassi would hit it back 80 MPH or more and the announcers would say, "He hit it back harder than it came", which is technically true. Now consider what a few more feet back can do to give you more time to play. Not only will the ball be going more slowly, but you will have more time simply because the ball had to travel further.

Biggest Problems, Biggest Solutions First

Similar to the idea of playing defense first on the first shot, you now must identify your opponent's main strategy, for winning points. On changeovers, when I coach college or high school, I ask these highly skilled players the following questions: How are you winning your points? How are they winning their points? How are you losing your points? How are they losing their points? There will be at least one salient answer to those questions. Most often we address having my player avoid losing points easily, and then also trying to mute the top weapon of the opponent, but playing more defensively.

Defense First

After the serve or return, having a defense-first mentality helps on all subsequent shots. There are different places from which you can find a better ability to mute your opponent's strong shot. Knowing what to expect from your opponent, recovering well into a good position, using effective strokes that don't easily get beat up by a suddenly fast shot, and knowing how to modify your strokes based on your position in the court, these things can help you defend well. Knowing how and where to send it back can sometimes take a time of discovery on the court. That's why tennis players are great problem solvers. Sometimes, you will play someone with the strangest shot you have ever seen in your life, and yes you have to hit it back. I have many stories, but I will tell just one.

Starting The Lawnmower

Maynard had a backhand that looked like he was trying to start a lawnmower, that was upside down, over his left shoulder. He hit a very strange shot, that corkscrewed way up in the air, about 10' above the net, and when it landed it jumped 3' to 5' to the left, which was very unsettling to his confused enemies. Because they never figured out how to deal with that shot, he won many matches, and this was not a technique that anyone would say they are proud to own or to have taught.

Weird-looking shots can be effective against lower-level players.

As his coach, I faced scorn for not having 'corrected' it. After two weeks of trying, I left that shot alone, because it was going to take too long to change it for the upcoming season, and the transition was not good for Maynard's confidence. Instead, we worked to make sure Maynard's backhand was as effective as could be. He learned to vary the amount of spin, then he was unbeatable at his position at #5 singles against not-so-strong players from other schools. Facing him, I would say that you need to learn to read the spin and take some final adjusting steps to get in great position to hit. What he does with that shot, makes all of that more difficult. All tennis players should strive to do likewise, make the opponent uncomfortable, out of position, off-balance, and create openings in the court.

Whose Weakness Is Most Important?

Remember, you are the second most important person on the court. It's very important to respond well to your opponent's strengths. Even more important is to explore their weaknesses, with your shot-making. Your shot tolerance increases, when you select the right shot, to mitigate their strength, and play to a weakness.

Chapter Twenty Seven

Why Isn't Receiving Taught?

Your receiving skills with the ball will speak directly to how well you play on the day. Those abilities determine your ability to defend the opponent's best shots. The two sentences above run completely counter to what many players, obsessed with technique, do. Instead, they think only about how to 'hit the shot back'. Moving into position is critical, and maintaining relatively low anxiety levels can also help. Peter was down 5-love to a player who was bigger and stronger and had a better serve and forehand. I first asked Peter to simply run down more balls, to get a racquet on them, because it would have been easy to give up. He lost the first set 6-1, which seems like a bad defeat until you understand, he split the last two games. Then I asked Peter to try to stay even, and that if he can get a few more balls, he can begin to frustrate his opponent, focusing on high percentage, and simply holding serve. The scores went 1-1,2-2,3-3,4-4, and you could see that the other player was hoping for a blowout set.

Impatience Can Help You

This happens often, a player winning the first set easily

does not expect the second set to be more difficult, and then they get frustrated. They can start thinking too much about the final score, and how they are going to brag about their quick win. This second set, though, went into a tiebreaker, which Peter won, when the other player tightened up and started to spray balls all over the court. Peter won the third set 6-1, as the other player imploded because he believed that he shouldn't even be in a third set. Peter's only change in play was to receive the ball as well as he could. At first, that meant changing winners to balls that he barely touched, then as he ramped up his effort he was able to reach more balls well, using the lob often.

Players who win an easy first set, can tighten up quickly if the second set gets more difficult.

Reacting Just Right

If you are not in position, either over, or under-reacting mentally, making catching the ball on your strings more difficult, that is where you should begin. Work on the fastest, yet smoothest reactions to the ball, and you will save a lot of time. In my lessons, I tell people, "You can react on time, or late, but there is no early", so the fastest possible smooth reaction is as close to on time as you will get. One of the tennis-teaching fads, that has come and gone is 'ball recognition', which should actually be fundamental teaching from every coach. Reading the ball out of the strings of your opponent is fundamental to helping you react quickly to the ball, and thus get in position. You simply can't have early reactions without full attention on to the stimulus. Viktor Frankl said, "In between stimulus and response, there is a moment of decision." The problem with tennis players is that they don't put enough effort into recognizing what stimuli are coming from the opponent's strings.

The Elements Of Tolerance

Shot tolerance takes a couple of different forms. 1. Being able to meet the incoming power with firmness. 2. Moving long distances quickly, making a smooth shot. 3. Accounting for the change in timing and ball bounce height from various spins. 4. Realizing that you don't have to meet power with power.

Now we will dig a bit more deeply into reading and reacting to the ball.

Chapter Twenty Eight

When Does Shot Tolerance Start?

Approximately 100% of players who come to me for a first lesson, do NOT accurately read and react to the ball coming out of my strings. I say approximately that percentage because there might have been one student who did, and maybe I forgot who that person was. Except for that one mythical player, everyone else fails to some degree in ball recognition. Almost immediately, when made aware of what they previously were not aware of, it reaps immediate results, in their ability to harvest each ball. Visual Training for Tennis addresses this in greater depth.

Shot Tolerance Begins At The Beginning

Reading and reacting to your opponent's shot, requires discipline, to bring your full attention, to that moment. The time to see is just before and right at the contact with the ball, by the player on the other side. You will most likely have to move quickly from unconscious incompetence, which means that you didn't know, you weren't seeing the ball, coming from the strings to conscious competence of that moment. In the short term, you will begin to train yourself, to mindfully see the ball coming out, now that you have entered conscious incompetence. The good news is, conscious incompetence doesn't last long, but it can feel painful for a few seconds. Move quickly to conscious competence, remind yourself often, to see the ball at opponent's contact until it becomes automatic. If you drive a car, you know the feeling, of the car seemingly driving itself, and you don't remember how you got home, because you were lost in thought. Apprehending the ball at the very beginning of its flight can be like that, with conscious practice, until you become unconsciously competent. Using a relaxed concentration approach is better than trying to focus during an entire point, I find that all that high effort focusing becomes quite fatiguing.

Give It A Try

The other piece to this competence is the physical performance of allowing all of your visual attention to be directed at the player and their swing. I'm guessing that as you read this you are saying to yourself, "I do that", but when I challenge you to say "hit", right at the moment the opponent hits the ball, you will find that you are doing extra, that you were not doing before, and that is when you will discover that you were not truly dialed into their contact point.

Changing Direction

As you know, hitting the ball back in the same direction it is coming from is the lowest risk shot you can attempt. The more often you change the direction, and size of the change of angle increases the likelihood that you will make an error. As you advance, you will need to develop this skill. But you will also need to develop good decision-making skills in regard to when is the best time to do it. Adjusting the direction of the ball requires better timing. To send it back with minimal angle change, all you need to do is meet the ball flush with strings facing back to the opposition. I do a drill with a ball machine, where I ask my players to hit the ball back at the ball machine, and also put a target or two nearby to create a target area with minimal angle change in the shot. After warm-up, I track their ability to hit the target area. When they have to change the direction of the ball to the other side, in the short term, their performance drops by 50%, but then they advance in this skill, and the percentage can increase. My best players will be able to be approximately 90% as accurate on balls that they changed angle. Changing direction will never be 100% as good as hitting back in the same direction the ball came.

The Safest Shot

The most conservative way to receive the ball is to lob it back. Lobbing is an essential tool to stay at a point. Lobs are under-utilized and under-practiced, mainly because of the strange stigma placed on the shot. If you lob a few times, you run the risk of being accused of being a 'lobber', one of the most despised players on a tennis court. Do you care about that? I don't. I want to win!

I hate lobbers. ~ Losing Tennis Player

Listen carefully to someone who says they hate lobbers because they just told you how to drive them nuts. Too many players have a misplaced sense of what counts in a match, but there are no judges, no subjective marks for having a good-looking game, there are only points won and points lost, and I like to win more and come out with the W. I am not a proponent of Winning Ugly, but I do agree that it's not a beauty contest. Think of it as winning intelligently. What power does someone have to question my manhood, if I just beat them? Instead of being the princess of the ball, or the prince of the low net skimming shot, look to be the gritty one who knows how to win. If you master the lob, you will make yourself 10-25% harder to beat immediately.

Lobs: Ultimate Shot Tolerance

Lobbing can be an effective way to win points, mostly because you are much less likely to make an error, once you get the range of your shot since you are sending the ball up in the air to have it come down anywhere from 45 degrees to even approaching 90 degrees to the court. Those angles open a very wide angle of acceptance into the court, much more than an 80 MPH shot hit at 17 degrees upward. Besides, there are different ways to hit the ball up in the air for different effects.

Master the lob and you will
become much harder to beat today

Offensive lobs are hit a bit lower and can have topspin, and are useful when the opponent is at the net. You want to make sure that you are in a good position, and make sure that your ball goes at least two feet over their outstretched racquet. Defensive lobs go higher and more advisable the more you are stretched out for a shot. The higher you hit it, the more time you get, to recover into the court, but be careful on a windy day, because the higher lobs in the wind can be blown out. Lobs also can be a great part of a two-shot combination, proceeded or followed by a drop shot. Now we will discuss the most basic staples of winning, knowing your A-game, and beginning to plan your B and maybe a C game strategy that you change to when you face a tough match-up.

Chapter Twenty Nine

Who Needs An A, B and C Game?

As we move along in our study, the material is more and more forward thinking. Higher level players will find more that they can do immediately, because they have been playing for years, but you newer players hang in there, because you want to catch a vision for where you are headed.

Pre-Planning A Framework For Development

Whether you are a coach, player or parent, and you are learning for yourself, your students, or wanting your children to play well, you want to start with a framework, a pathway to success. If your game lacks organization and/or direction, it's easy to get stuck in the quagmire of apocryphal wisdom out there. One of the most important things is to start with a framework for strategy, one that suits you, your personality, skill set, and physique. In this way you create a pathway for learning. This protects you from losing a match, having 'bad' backhands, then taking a lesson on backhand. What you really should do is look at how to get more forehands, and then do a little work on your backhand. When you work on what the final outcome will be, you are less likely to do patchwork on your game.

Where Are You Headed?

Steven Covey in his book 7 habits of highly effective people, says "Begin with the end in mind". When the final destination, or a few final destinations to choose from are offered, then the path along the way becomes more clear. Once that understanding is established, the why and wherefore of each objective along the way, has something to connect to in the mind of the player, executing the plan. Creating a mind map of the finished product is important. One example of this is a newish player, RJ, who in the next year wants to make his varsity team when he is a freshman. I recently discovered something about him, similar to a small minority of players, he seems very much prone to hitting the ball relatively flat, even so we began to work on some topspin in his game. He may never play like Nadal, and I am hard pressed to find a pro comparison for his pre-disposition. He does remind me of some other very good players, Aaron and Preston, I have coached in the past. How they played creates a template for me, from which to work with RJ, who will also have a lot of say so in how he develops his game.

It takes a long time to learn to play like yourself.
~ Miles Davis

Everyone needs a coach, and my job in that role is to know the way, go the way and show the way. His job is to give me the feedback I need to help him decide, and his parents are also another vital pair of eyes and ears in regard to their son's development. RJ's ultimate destination is his own creation. None of this is done in a vacuum, and there are few successful lone rangers. Even Federer, when he didn't have a coach, still consulted with top experts, in particular areas, to develop his game.

Understanding The Pathway

A player like RJ needs to understand their pathway, how that differs from other players, with differing talents and predispositions. All of this is a foreshadowing of learning to play like yourself. Without this lighting of the way, each learning task seems like a mystery in a dark tunnel, the player does not know why they are doing this, but they blindly follow along.

The Ingredients Of Your ABC

The fact that no matter what strategies are, your A, B and C game might be, your ability to hit targets on the court are paramount to success, and yet few coaches, parents or players consider that as a regular part of training, instead focusing on the look, of the form of the shot. The vast majority of professional players have extremely small targets that they practice hitting for extended periods of time.

Avoid Obsession With Technique

Most players get more and more obsessed with technique, instead of how they play the ball. This means you can gain a huge advantage, by studying the tactics of the relatively brainless performer. They fantasize about instinctively playing a match like their top tennis heroes, but they have no real game plan, and many times make the most fundamental mistakes. Imitating a particular move from an iconic player is not a bad idea, unless it's something that doesn't work for you, then it is a terrible concept.Playing a style that doesn't fit you is like wearing shoes that are too small, or full size too big, it's going to hurt! On the other hand, research shows, when you do watch top players, it's proven that you will play better next time out, but it doesn't mean you have to try to imitate them perfectly. Studies seem to indicate, that your brain will adapt the information for you, and I have seen this proven over again in real life.

Build Your A, B and C One Shot At A Time

When you are experimenting with how to play the ball, search for technical solutions to tactical problems. Learn one shot at a time, or how to return one shot at a time. Recently Mark came out for a lesson because in his 3.0-3.5 flex league, there are some slicers and dicers, total hacks who are not going much further, but are not easy to beat, at that level. We worked not only on his own slice shot, but how to hit a myriad of different slices to the side that was troubling him most, the forehand. He also learned how to take all of those shots, turning them into deep cross-court shots. Add nuance to your strength, or shore up a weakness, and you will get 1% more effective very quickly. There is more to gain from developing a new tactic from your strength, then there is from obsessing about a perceived weakness in your game. The better you get at attacking, the less time you spend on defense. A good offense also helps you on your defense. This might seem to contradict what was discussed earlier. The concept is that we always think defense first, but if you are never offensive, you will be under attack more, conversely when you start to attack more, putting the other player on defense, then you will feel less pressure, and thus have great shot tolerance. Strategy and targets go hand in hand, forming the basis for developing the tactics. that build on your ideal strategic foundation. All of these things are based on who you are, your present skills, predispositions, and your relative talent level. After that, your direction is created by what you want to become as a player, and what is realistically a great fit for you.

Your Strokes Look So Nice

I remember a time when I had very technically sound strokes, and people liked watching me play, because my technique was pleasing to the eye, even as I lost winnable matches. I often lost to players whose racquet work was loaded with idiosyncratic motions. This was very frustrating, so I can relate to those who have struggled with that scenario.

It can feel frustrating and demoralizing to lose to people who seemingly are non-athletes, or have strange-looking techniques, but that's the reason for this book, to give you the foundational tools to build a winning game. You can also raise the floor of your lowest performances, becoming more error-proof. You won't have to worry about losing, because you had a less intelligent approach, in fact, you likely will begin to beat people who seem to have superior athleticism and strokes.

Chapter Thirty

What Is My Bread And Butter Shot?

The geometry of a tennis court is deceptive because the court is full of rectangles, but the ball almost always flies on a diagonal, and playing diagonal shots is where the intelligent play can be found, with a few exceptions, which will be covered in more depth in Tennis Strategy 201. The ball is an arcing, bouncing, spinning, grabbing, sliding object. It moves, hits the ground, and then based on the reaction of the ball with the ground it's gonna do something different every time. As Master Pro Ken DeHart says, "Every ball is a question, do you have the answer?" It can curve toward you or away from you, are you ready to adjust accordingly to accept the ball?

The game is played with curves, arcs and triangles. One definite truth is that if you hit crosscourt there are 82.5 feet along the hypotenuse of the court, instead of 78' along its length. You gain four and a half more feet or the width of a doubles alley. People overstate the idea that the net is lower in the middle because if you are closer to the line, then hitting straight ahead over the closer net is the same obstacle as going over a further obstacle that is marginally lower.

The Court Is 78', But Can
Play As Though It Is Longer

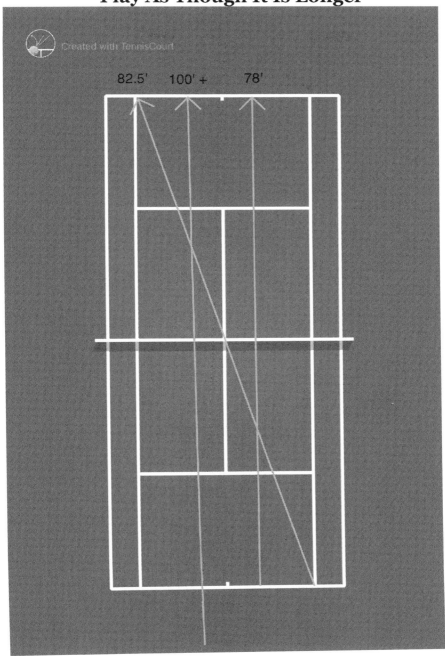

Playing the full length of the court crosscourt gives the best blend of offense and defense.

When you play any kind of strategic game from chess to monopoly to any card game you might play, playing offense is important, playing defense is more important, but playing a shot that is both offensive and defensive is ideal, and the way to be most effective. Overly offensive players become vulnerable to counterattack, or making errors. The deep crosscourt shot pushes your opponent farther from the net, increasing the chance they will miss, decreasing the chance that they can hit an offensive shot back to you. You then stretch them to a limit of shot tolerance and thus increase your own. They will be unwise to significantly change the direction of the shot because if they do, they open up many more options for you. It's ok to be predictable in this way.

"You are so predictable."
"Be quiet, I'm still beating you."

I had a fun experience training an aspiring top junior from Romania, who ended up being selected to his college's athletic hall of fame. During our training when he was only 13, we would play practice matches, and he would challenge me and complain after a point, "You are so predictable, I knew you were going cross court." I responded, "Be quiet, I am still beating you." I went on to explain that being unpredictable is fine, as long as you don't give up tactical advantage. By his desire to be tricky, he gave me too many down-the-line shots, which opened up offensive opportunities for me. I gave him very few opportunities, which lead to more for me.

Deep Shots

On the other hand, if you hit the service line on the other side or shorter, you will face much more pressure on your shots, thus increasing the challenge level to ward off your opponent's pressuring shots. Your time and space will be under attack as your opponent is provided easy power by moving forward into the shot. Your movement will also be under attack if you go for down-the-line shots too early in the rally and your opponent successfully changes the direction of your shot crosscourt. So wait until you have a legitimate shot at winning the point before going down the line.

Chapter Thirty One

Why Hit Deep Up The Middle?

Once players on tour saw how dominating the Williams sisters both were when they were allowed to run all over the court, almost universally players would do their best to keep them in the center. Conversely, both Williams' learned to control the center of the court. One of my favorite matches to watch, was a slightly out of form Venus Williams, beating Victoria Azarenka, simply playing very gritty, keeping the ball very slightly cross-court deep. It was a brainy tactical win, but it did not look impressive for sheer technical prowess, as Azarenka was not able to fight her way out of the center of the court well enough to create offense. Venus took that in three tough sets.

Think Of It As 'Caging', Or Quicksand

Styrling Strother calls this 'caging' a player, and I like the word because they can feel trapped. That would be runner, is then stuck in the middle. They likely will find it difficult to accelerate into a run, when you do make them run. You can make them feel like they are standing in quicksand, which really should be called slow sand. Going up the middle well, directly at the player, causes them to have to get out of the way of your shot. When you attack them in this way, it can jam them causing errors. At the very least you can reduce the volume of offense they can muster from this compromised position. This is a tactic that is happening more and more on the pro tour, and there is no reason you can't do it too. Good returners are hitting returns back to the server's forehand side in B and trying to jam them and keep them from hitting a very good S +1 shot, (The Next Shot After The Serve).

Safety Of Your Shot

One great benefit of attempting to place the ball up the middle, for the newer player, is that if you were to miss by 5', 10' or even 13.5', then the ball still can go in the court. In certain circumstances, going deep down the middle is safer than cross-court. Consider also, if you are going for a deep cross-court shot, and you happen to be a bit late on the shot, you can get a deep center shot.

Stefan Plays The Game Plan

One of the greatest matches I have witnessed one of my players playing was not a win, but he gave himself a chance against a top player playing 6.0 level tennis. My #92 ranked player played the #1 player in NorCal in a high school sectional playoff match, a player who had a full-ride scholarship to the University of California, Berkeley waiting for him. Going into the match no one gave my player a chance. They thought it would be two easy sets, maybe 6-0, 6-0. Even I would have been satisfied if he won a few games, but I always start a match thinking that it can be won because that's the only way you can win. I had to convince my team to believe in miracles. Thai, the #1 was perhaps the fastest high school tennis player I had ever seen. Stefan's game plan was to keep him in the center of the court. He also planned to go for winners and accepting forcing errors on every short ball from Thai. He would do that by hitting it as hard as he could because that's the only way he was going to win points against this defensively gifted competitor. Using this tactic of pressuring Thai's time and space, he was able to keep Thai from generating power, and also created openings for winners. If the whole match had been a track meet, Thai would have kept Stefan off balance, and with few openings, generating power on the move was his strength.

Stefan Kept Thai From Moving
As Much As He Prefers

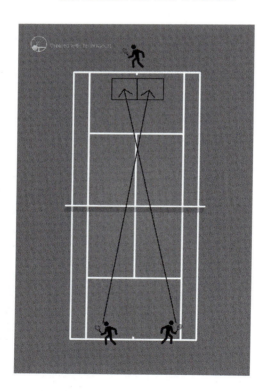

As the match progressed, Thai won the first set 6-3, but Stefan's game plan was getting more and more effective. From down 2-1 and a break in the second, I asked Stefan to play the best tennis of his life, he nodded once, then came back to win the second set 6-4, before fitness and experience took over and he lost 6-1 in the third set, but not before Thai recognized this as the most difficult match he ever played in high school.

By keeping the ball ever so slightly cross-court, and not allowing Thai to change the direction of the ball, run, or move forward on short balls, Stefan gave himself a chance to win.

Chapter Thirty Two

How Do I Win At Percentage Tennis?

95% of matches are won by the player who wins 51% of the points in the match. Think about that, it means that the opponent won only 49%, so that's a 2% swing. 99% of matches are won by the player who wins 55% of the points. Interestingly enough, when you look at the statistics at the end of the year, a dominant player will have an overall win percentage of 55%, a player with a 54% might still be the number one player in the world, but the #2 player may also have that same percentage. 80% of matches are won by the player who simply wins ONE MORE POINT. At this writing, Rafa Nadal is 15-0 on the year winning 57% of his points.

Coming From Behind

Consider that you can lose more points and have a 1 in 5 chance of winning the match. In that case, you need to win the breakpoints, and not allow your opponent to win them as often. So, fight and claw for every point you can, and you may be able to be the exception.

A Bad Set, Or A Few Bad Games

If you lose 2% more points, in the match, it might be because you had a significantly rough patch in the match, recovered, and then in the decisive parts of the match you performed well. Perhaps the opponent played very well, then cooled off. Even so, if you have a margin of 2% you are trying to overcome, then you are only going to win 1 in 20, so you better play better, to turn it around. Some of the crazier stories in tennis are after a player has lost the first set 6-0, and is behind in the second, before something major clicks or the other player tightens, and they go on to win a close match at the end. Those are 1 in 100 types of wins. While many people love the idea of the scrappy underdog, the main point is, TO WIN MORE POINTS.

Fight Until The Bitter End

Be the one who has a better chance to win, but always realize that you still have a chance until they win the final point. I have won double digits matches in my life coming back from match point down. So can you. I can't remember how many times I lost a match having had match point, but it wasn't often. You must respect your opponent, until you have won the final point, shake hands, and they put their racquet back in the bag. In high school play, I have seen more times than I would like, a player who was a game, or even a point away from winning, relaxed, lost intensity, and the other player came back to win.

Gain An Advantage In Every Game

The player who wins the first point of the game, has a 60% chance of winning it, slightly more if they are the server, and slightly less if you are the returner. This means you want to play your highest percentage play on the first point, so it's imperative to make your first serve or return the ball in the court. Unless you are a pure power player, this is not the time to hit your hardest serve, instead, you want the one that goes in more often. Flip it around, as a returner you might want to send the very first return back at the server, and no place else, because that is the safest return.

Become Tough To Beat

The best way to have a great chance at winning the point is not to lose it quickly. Besides, you want the opponent to know, they have to work for the points, you aren't just going to hand it to them. Billy Martin, the controversial and highly successful manager of the New York Yankees and Oakland A's, used to say, "You can't catch a walk." He wanted his pitchers to throw strikes, even if it meant the batter might hit the ball. A ball in play can be caught and the runner was thrown out. That means it's better to allow them to play, so that you can run it down than to miss, and lose automatically. Trust your defense!

Early Shot Direction

Another way to avoid putting yourself in a bad position is to avoid hitting the ball down the line too early in a point. Yesterday I was playing someone 15 years younger than me, who had also played at a higher level. You better believe I kept the ball crosscourt. When you hit the down the line too early you allow your opponent to put you under pressure right away. If they go cross-court, it makes your recovery more difficult. Hitting the ball too short early in the point also opens up opportunities for your antagonist. The first point is a great time to reestablish that deep cross-court combination of defense and offense, and first shots are the best way to do that. Start them further back in the court, they will be less likely to win the initial point.

The Race To 30

80% of points are won by the player who gets to 30 first. Of course, 30-love is better than 30-15, and 30-love for the server is stronger than for the returner, but win that race to 30. Styrling Strother, of The Art of Winning, has found that that player winning two straight points is very likely to lose the next point. That's a great time to recognize that when you are going for the 3rd straight point, you might want to play it the same way as the first point of a game. In addition, Styrling has discovered that players who win two straight points first win a high percentage of the games, and the player that wins three straight points more often in a match is much more likely to come out on top. Check out The Art of Winning Tennis, which is a collaboration between Dan Travis and Styrling. They are good friends of mine.

Hammering It Home

One way you can make your game more attack-proof is to play a game, where you develop a mindset of building the point cross-court, like warming up with scales, before playing a tune. In my pre-match mantra, before team matches, we always say

Build your points crosscourt, then wait for a down the line or short ball before getting creative.

Practice Point Construction Habits

One cooperative exercise that you can do with a friend, your team, or anyone that you practice with, is to do a timed game, where you serve, the server returns, and you execute a certain number of cross-court shots. The serve is automatically cross-court, they all are, but it's better if you hit it to the far corner, because that's a better cross court. The returner must make the return at least slightly cross-court, which is defined as crossing the center line in the court.* Typically, when I work with competitive players, we will play the game for 11 minutes, at first, each pair gets a point when they cooperatively execute a serve, return, and one more shot each cross court. They can get two points if they can also make two more shots, cross-court then the server serves again. Another variation is that you can count the return, and they end on an odd number of shots, the serve plus four consecutive cross-court shots, then the other player serves the next ball. It's tempting to want to play the point out to completion, but that's not the objective of the game. Instead, you want to accumulate points by establishing cross-court play. When first played, it will seem like a struggle to get a few points, but with a little time and practice you will get it down. Later, we shorten it to 9 minutes, 7 minutes, then 5 minute games. My highest level players might play quick rotations of 3 minutes which requires great concentration. The most important concept is that no one should try to win the point! With lower-level players, you might want to allow one shot to be played after two bounces one time per attempt, just to help build confidence. When confidence is established kick off the training wheels.

If you have multiple players playing this, you can rotate

among players, accumulate points and see who the big winner is. Each player should strive to make the others around them better.

It's a great game to play with everyone. As we said before, deep crosscourt shots are a staple of any major strategy you want to play. When playing strategically, some of those shots are technically centered shots, but you don't want to be too critical in the early going of playing the game.

Chapter Thirty Three

What Are The 5 Major Strategies?

The Power Player

The best way to hit a winner, force and error, or open the court is with a hard shot cross court. In the progression of Control, Hurt, Finish, the deep cross court shot could end up being anyone of the three, but maybe it's more likely to be a hurt shot, that gives you the opening for the next shot. Hitting pretty hard cross court is safer, then you get a weak shot, so your cross-court shot becomes the hurt shot, drawing out a short shot, then you get to move forward, you've got an opening, for you can go down the line for a winner.

One of the rules that I learned way back when from Allen Fox, in Think To Win, rally cross court and attack down the line. The more subtle part is to make sure you have an attackable ball for that line hugger. For the aggressive player, that steady pounding of cross-court shots earns you the right to go for a winner, when you get a short ball. Another interesting effect of going for deep angled shots is that you will sometimes get that accidental ball, placed a bit more into the corner and it forces an error or even becomes a winner you didn't even intend to hit. When they say nice shot, say thank you and don't admit that you didn't mean it. This can also set up an opportunity to hit a shorter angle to the other side which can make them run 32 feet, instead of 27, adding a few more feet enhances the offensive outcomes of that shot, that's a lot when you consider that a full stride can be 3 feet, you might make them take two full strides more to get the ball. Which leads us to pressure their movement.

Pressuring Movement

If you are not blessed with a ton of power, or the player on the other side is a better power play, one of your first options is to pressure their movement. Of course, this requires you to be a good mover on court. When pressuring movement, you want to start with serves to the corner, or returns crosscourt so that you set up the lateral and diagonal running game. You can also serve to the T and then hit behind the player, which creates tight quarters movement, which can make them feel constricted. As a returner, returning at them to 'cage' them, then going cross-court away from them many times makes them feel like they are trying to step out of quicksand. For instance, a serve to the T in the deuce court where they have to hit a backhand return, if they're a righty, then you turn them around to hit a forehand, going the other way, causing them to rotate in a tight space, creating positional challenge.

Pressuring Time And Space

The cross-court shot is a staple of increased pressure on time and space, because a good one creates a demand to move sideways, and maybe diagonally backward for a shot.

They will have to go quickly to hit a running forehand. The chances that they're going to execute as well, compared to when they are not under any pressure are not as good for them. Conversely, if you're hitting short balls, in the center of the court, you're not pressuring their time and space, they have a great chance to take away yours.

Another great way to take away time and space is to approach the net, the out wide serve is a great way to open the court for a serve and volley, but that might be something you learn to do in the future. Coming to the net on an approach from your forehand to their backhand has been found by Craig O'Shannessy is the most effective way to come to the net in a rally. Using an inside out forehand (from the center of the court) to their backhand not only gives the advantage of a few more MPHs, but also puts them under pressure to most likely have to use their worst shot to hit a demanding show, NOW! One element of using time and space is creating the requirement in their mind of the need to hit an important shot immediately. This runs counter to some conventional wisdom, that I had maintained in my mind that approach shots are much more effective down the line. You can still hit a forehand down the line to the backhand for an approach, or even a backhand to the forehand, although you don't want to do that as much, it can help make the other two approaches more effective. Very rarely would you ever want to hit a true cross-court approach shot, because the opening in which the passing shot can go is wide enough for a truck to drive through with room to spare? But as a crazy surprise shot it can be used once or twice per match. It has a way of disrupting the other player, but now we will look at that as a major strategy.

Disrupting Rhythm

Rafa Nadal, I do believe is capable of any strategy, but his main way of playing is mis-categorized, and misunderstood. Most analysts see him as a grinder. He is perhaps the most effective disrupter of rhythm for other players that have ever played the game. What is easily noticed about his propensity for hitting heavy topspin bouncing high to his counterpart's backhand? When you see him live in 3D, instead of on the 2D of a screen, you see something a bit more difficult to detect. When you see him in person, you can see how differently he takes cuts at the ball. Rafa rarely intentionally hits the ball the same way. Throughout his career he has also included many more flatter shots to penetrate the court to also shorten the points a bit. However, against most opponents, he is hitting that big bouncing shot above the shoulder of the other player. Also, he varies the arc of the ball, the amount of spin, so that the ball arrives in a different place, pace and space. This creates difficulty in positioning and timing for the other player. You might notice that he struggles a bit against tall players who are strong on the left side because they have a great two-handed backhand or are left-handed.

Retrieving Rally Player

Being a retrieving baseline player should be a last resort. You just have to run around and hit one more shot, but that can be very tiring. It's foolish for you to hit the ball down the line a lot, because you will create even more running for yourself. Even though you've resigned yourself to running around and just hitting one more shot, you have to reduce the amount of running to some degree, not add to it. I will caution you only to go down th e line if your opponent will not get there in time to change the direction of their shot.

Instead keep most everything deep cross-court, because that will make you harder to beat. Those shots will put your opponent in positions where it's harder for them to hit a winner against you.

Cross-court plays into every major strategy!
If somebody has a sixth category of strategy
I would love to hear your ideas about what it is.

Chapter Thirty Four

What Is Control,
Hurt and Finish?

The priority is to control the point, don't lose fast.
The next priority is to try to hurt your opponent
with spin, movement or speed of shot.
Finally, when you have earned a chance
to finish, do so, it could mean forcing
an error, or getting a winner.

Nick Bolletieri has a great phrase that every player should know and understand. The most important thing to know is that it's not a finite plan, but it does point to opportunities to achieve different things in a match. The phrase is Control, Hurt, Finish. You must control your first two shots, but if you place them well, and they then hurt your opponent or finish the point, that's a great unintended consequence. When you have an opportunity to make your opponent run a great distance, jam them, or push them way back in the court, you can hurt them enough that they may cough up a weak shot. That's what the hurt is all about, getting something attackable. If those shots happen to finish the point, so be it, but your main objective should be to force a weak shot, so you can finish with the next shot.

Winners Are Not Sustainable

The trap inexperienced players fall into is that they accidentally hit a winner, or they accidentally hurt their opponent early in the point, then they ditch the control the point method. In a search for more gratification, they shift to playing more risky shots, with not enough reward.

Chapter Thirty Five

The Warm-Up Is How Long?

I know the pain of pulling into the parking lot about one minute before my match starts, running in, checking in, going right on the court warm-up after a two-hour drive. It doesn't work very well, as you can imagine.

The five-minute warm-up is not a good name, because you should warm up much longer and earlier for your match. A minimum amount of warm-up time hitting on the court should be about 15 minutes, as you want to divide that up minimally between 5 minutes of groundstrokes, 5 minutes of volleys, and 5 full minutes of serving. When I am coaching a team, I want my players all on court 30 full minutes before the match. That way they can get 10 minutes of groundstrokes, 5 minutes of volleys, 5 minutes of lobs, and overheads, followed by 5 full minutes of serves before we have our pre-game talk. Your warm-up should also include some programmed self-talk to prep yourself for what you want to accomplish on the day. If you fail to plan, maybe planning to fail. How many times do players go play a match, almost completely forgetting what they wanted to do, then kick themselves later? That's the pain I used to feel. During the five-minute scouting time, you should hit your opponent's balls to their forehand and backhand, study how they hit. Then give them high, low, and medium balls and see which ones they struggle with, and which ones they hit very well. Try slightly different speeds, and maybe some different spins. Try to find their favorite shot and their weakest shot.

Tournament

When you are going to a tournament, especially if you have never been there before, you most likely want to arrive an hour early. That way, if you take a wrong turn or some other major road disruption happens, you can still arrive 45 minutes before your match. When you arrive, go take a look at all the courts, look for some of the interesting unique features of the place. Will balls bounce off of walls? Are there low fences, netting between courts, courts in good, bad, or varying condition?

Before you even leave, scout out some local courts close to the facility, in case they have no courts for warming up. If that is simply not available, then you can go through a physical warm-up of a light jog, some core work, working some rubber tubing, medicine balls, and some stretching. You can do some shadow swings, and warm up your serving shoulder with some nice light swinging. Sit and visualize yourself starting the match playing well, finishing, shaking hands with the win. There could be a flat space somewhere to hit some mini groundstrokes, or some volleys back and forth with someone on site. Surely someone wants to feel the ball in their racquet. If I had a dollar for every time I warmed up in the corner of a parking lot, I would take you out to lunch all week. When you are on-site, most clubs give you a full run of the place, but be sure to check before you go for a swim, get in the hot tub, etc. I worked a club where players were expected to stay in the tennis area or locker room at all times.

Flex League

These matches will largely be played at parks, but some at clubs. Most likely, the club is not rolling out the red carpet, so try not to arrive ahead of your opponent by much, because you could get the "And you are...?" treatment. Be sure to communicate with your opponent about what the arrangements are. They should have reserved a court, just as you should when you host. The amount of warm up time will be negotiated between the two of you. It's good to get that out early, but you are most likely running up against limited court time, so see the above rules for tournament play.

Your Buddy

It's great to find a friend for practice matches. In this case, make sure you get a very full warm-up. Depending on whether you might want to get a full 30 minutes in before playing a set. Run a few drills, play a few cooperative games. One of the most interesting things you can do is rally after the match, you might find that you are playing at a higher level after the 'pressure' of the match is relieved. This can be a part of what helps you get to a higher level, as you learn to play in a more relaxed fashion. Another thing to consider is to make some practice match rules, like he will give you short balls to attack approach shots, and you will play a lot of balls to his backhand so he can practice in live match play. This way the outcome of the match is not so important, but you are achieving some objectives. Another way to do this is to take turns serving 6 or 8 serve points, then rotating as though it was a service game, this way the tyranny of the score is not there, and you can focus more on what you are practicing.

Playing Tiebreakers

Playing tiebreakers is necessary if you are going to win them later. Don't call your opponent lucky if she wins the tiebreaker, especially if she practices them and you don't.

Chapter Thirty Six

How Do I Get Off To A Good Start?

It's time to spin the racket. Once the spin of the racquet happens there are four choices for the winner. 1. Serve 2. Receive. 3. Side To Start On 4. Make The Opponent Choose First (Do this if you want to control the side). If they choose the shady side, you will receive first, then you will serve on the shady side, and they will be first to serve on the sunny side. You should have already decided after hitting your serves what you want to do when the spin of the racquet occurs. Part of the body language of a match is confidently choosing what you will do. Whatever you do, choose it with certainty and a smile. Nothing says a lack of full confidence, like "Oh well, oh yeah, I guess I'll serve." There are different ways to approach this, and it's a good idea to have some basic ideas of how you will make your decision. In most circumstances, I want to serve first, because I am confident and proactive, and knowing that I can hold serve, I will likely take the lead and in best cases, not relinquish it. What will cause me to want to return serve?

First Round Jitters, Tightness, Weird Conditions Like Wind, My Opponent Looks Nervous, My Warm Up Serves Did Not Go Well, I'm Not Feeling Warmed Up Yet

Maybe you have had a hard time getting off to a good start, then you want to return first, because it's not as bad to lose a game on their serve to start a match as it is to lose your serve, because you will then be down a break, immediately. But, if you look at the list above and you see your opponent exhibiting any of those, you might want to be extra sure to let them serve first.

Are you more of an aggressive player, or more of a counter puncher, if your return game is stronger than your service game, then be the returner. When your opponent forces you to serve first, be sure to check the sun, to make sure you calculate that they will serve on the worst side first.

While it doesn't make sense, because no one is in the lead until they get up a break, there is a psychological advantage to always being in the lead.   1-0, 2-1, 3-2, can have your opponent feeling like they are playing catch up. When you decide to return, realize that you are not in the lead until you break, and are not behind until you are broken. When you see that your opponent looks vulnerable on serve and you can break them in the first game, as long as you keep up good play, you may be able to break their spirit if you break them again.

Chapter Thirty Eight

How Do I Manage Momentum?

One of the horrible recent developments is the default position that matches are played as best of two sets with a 10 point TB to decide the match. The Match TB. Most of us purists hate that as a dumbing down of the sport, which reduces a match to a level where fitness is not a deciding factor like it once was. In a two or three-hour match, you find out who did the work and deserves to win. In best of two, you only need one set and a few weird points in a tiebreak. Even so, there is a strategy if that is the situation that you are forced to accept. There is one benefit to the two-set matches, and it's that of being able to finish the match in good time. One of the strangest phenomena is that of playing a tiebreaker to get into a tiebreaker, I call it 'breaker for the breaker'.

Short Term Momentum Dynamic

To succeed with tiebreakers you have to understand the momentum dynamic. There is a proven effect that happens after you win a set. You get a bit of a dopamine response, your blood pressure and heart rate drop, so then you lose some intensity. So, when you win a set, then you also need to reset your mind and do all you can to get your heart rate back up and get your intensity for the beginning of the second set, or you can find yourself down 3-0 in about five minutes. Your aim should be to win both sets, then you don't have to face the jeopardy of a tiebreaker. Another thing that happens often is that a player will overcome a deficit in a set, like coming back from 4-1 down to make it 5-all, celebrate, lose intensity, and the set 7-5, just like that.

Feeling Of Relief

Or they get relieved that they made it into a tiebreaker, but then they feel pressure again, tighten up, and next thing you know they are down 4-1 or 5-0 in the TB. I don't have any hard data on this, but I have seen it many times. If I had to guess I would say it happens about 70% of the time, that people have a dip in play either because intensity dropped, or they felt too much pressure.

Mounting Pressure

When people win the second set to force a match tiebreak, this same type of thing happens. More experienced players are not as much affected by this, but everyone can be helped by the following strategy. Consider the tiebreaker to be a part of the second set. It takes a little mental construction to create this reality. When you think about it, if you had won the first set, and then lost the second if you win the TB, you win the match, so what's wrong with saying it's still part of the second set, and you get a second chance to win it. Turn that around now, if you won the second set, keep yourself from getting excited, tell yourself that you indeed have not won the second set, until you win the tiebreaker. Whoever wins the second set wins the match. I have yet to coach a player who didn't use this effectively to play well in the finishing stage of the match. They didn't win them all, but then they also didn't suffer from a huge dip in play at the worst possible time. I believe that the winner of the second set seems to lose the tiebreaker about 70% of the time, and maybe more if they had to play 'the breaker for the breaker', because of the emotions behind eking out a close set.

16 Second Cure

More importantly, there is a 16-second cure, developed by Jim Loehr, who is one of the top sports psychologists in the world. There are up to 4 things you can do between points to keep yourself playing closer to your best and be less affected by negative or positive points. 1. Make sure you end that point in your mind, it's over. Nothing you can do about it anymore. 2. Go through a moment of relaxation, taking a few seconds to take a deep breath or two is part of it. 3. Review the previous point objectively if needed, then plan your next point. 4. Go into your rituals, so that you have some control over something in the match.

Protect Against Ups And Downs

If you practice the 16-second cure, and get good at it, it becomes a sort of inoculation against dips in performance throughout the match. Sometimes when people talk about being 'consistent', I think what they partially mean is that they don't want to have huge ups and downs in their play from point to point, game to game, set to set. You want to determine that you will give 100 percent effort on every point.

Closure

The way the 16-second cure works is that immediately after a point ends, you got through phase 1, where you end the point in your mind, and your body language says a lot about how well you do that. you do something physical to mark the end of that point. You might turn away, do a fist pump, slap your leg, something that says, "that point is done". There is nothing you can do about it now. That takes maybe two seconds or less.

Relax

Then you go into relaxation, take a deep breath, scan your body for tension, let it go. You might shake out your arms like a noodle and do a languid walk. From there, once you have cleared your mind...

Plan

take a quick look back on what just happened during that point, was there anything you can learn from it? That might take a few seconds, but then you have to go forward to think about the score and how you want to play the next point. Make a plan. From there you have to have some contingencies, and...

Ritual

You can go into the ritual that you do before returning or serving that is always the same. This gives you feelings of control over something in the match. `thing really helps with maintaining intensity so you know just point to point let your effort be you know close to 100 and you won't have the same types of issues so but just realize um you know in fact one of the best things i ever learned i was i was an assistant coach for a college team and um and the head coach had a little saying that he wanted to see all of his players you know play with maximum intensity for the first two games of the set and then take it from there so so there was this sort of this checking in this reset at the beginning of a match to really make sure am i giving full intensity and then you don't have these dips in play where you know you win a set and then all of a sudden you find yourself down three love in the second because you know there was like a lucky shot on a three-all ball and then and then you know you played a bad game or whatever and now you're down three love two breaks and that's that's a tough thing to come back from so in general you got to learn these things about the mental emotional psychological physiological ups and downs of a match by thinking about them and practicing them and having a strategy for them.

Chapter Thirty Nine

Do Good People Finish First?

Don't worry so much about your reputation, because that's simply what others think about you, instead consider your character, because that is who you are.
~ John Wooden

One thing that can help you a lot is to build your game around fair play. I don't know how many times my grandfather told me, "It's not whether you win or lose, it's how you play the game." I thought he was crazy, but now I know the value of ethics and etiquette. Being a person who is enjoyable to play against is a sure way to help advance your game, as then people will want to play with you again later.

Prioritize The Social Aspect Of Playing The Game To Build Your Social Community That Will Also Advance Your Game.

Integrity Is A Strategy

This is a strategy and you know it's an interesting thing because this obviously has nothing to do with x's and o's. It can be foundational because as a new player you want to get well plugged into the tennis community. Your initial play should be as much about making friends and finding practice partners. Determining that you will make good calls, wins and loses graciously, and treats every with respect for their time and their person. It also can be a part of your mental game.

Play fair, be reasonable, exhibit great sportsmanship, and have fun. Keep in mind, it still is just a game, even though you want to win.

When you play fair, then you know you deserve to win, but when you are a jerk or a cheater, then you will always wonder if you were good enough. If you love the sport, then honor it accordingly, and expect everyone you play to do so. Success is not guaranteed, but deserving it is! If someone cheats you and you cheat them back, then you are no better. "The Code" for tennis says that if you are not sure about a call, you should call it good, and a ball that is 99% out, is 100% good. About 95% of players will call the ball fairly, but maybe not that high in competitive junior tennis which has an epidemic of cheating at this time.

How To Handle Bad Calls

When it comes to someone making bad calls against you, there are ways to handle that gracefully. First, consider that learning to make good calls takes some time and experience and that a person's anxiety level, may also affect their visual acuity. Some people want to win so badly, that they get a sort of psychological blindness, and their brain tells them the ball was out because they want it to be. Far fewer people are criminal in their calls and will call the ball out on breakpoint, because it was on the line. If you treat everyone as though they sincerely want to give good calls, that's a nice philosophy. If a player makes what you think was a bad call, remember, they are closer to the ball. But if you do disagree, simply give them a doubtful look, look at the line, then look at them again. You are giving a strong non-verbal signal that you don't agree. Sometimes, that player will see that action, and offer, "Did you think that was in?", and when you say yes, they then give you the point. You make a friend that way, you learn that you can trust them. Most people will just move on as though nothing happened. If they make another bad call, then you can say, "Pat, are you sure about that call?", which crudely translated means, "Pat, I think you missed that call." Almost 100% of the time that player will say they are sure, but now you have seen two instances, and you also put them on notice. You did that by using their name, which disempowers them from feelings of anonymity. If they make another bad call, and it's a tournament, then you can get a linesperson. If it's not a match where officials are present, you may have to express to your opponent that you now have disagreed with three calls, and you hope there are not anymore. Be gentle, because they might have a vision problem. Vision is a tricky thing and people because the anxiety of the match, gets to them they might not be seeing as well.

What Happens Next At A Tournament

Whether they are making mistakes or they are outright trying to steal the match from you, play the game ethically. You can leave the court to go find an official or go back to the tournament desk to let them know that you need one. You are responsible to keep playing until a linesperson can be found. In extreme cases where bad calls continue in this period, you may want to play very slowly, or stop if the conditions are unbearable.

What Happens Next In High School Play

Talk to your coach about what the policy is for getting a linesperson. In most leagues, getting a linesperson must be initiated by a player, although who knows if a coach prods a player to request one. You owe it to your team to request one because the player cheating you are also cheating your team.

What Happens Next In Flex League

You are at the mercy of the opponent in the short term, but if you get to that third call that they have missed, it's best to be firm, but fair. Avoid insults about their vision or their ethics. Stick to the case at point, you disagree with their calls. It's ok to voice that, and you can ask them to be more careful with them. If you see another missed call you can tell them where you saw it. Keep in mind there was a time when I questioned a few of my player's calls in practice matches, both players thought I was nuts and over-reaching, and then it turned out I needed glasses for the first time in my life. I was probably 5 years overdue for glasses. So, before you start getting too uppity, make sure you get your own eyes checked.

What Happens Next In USTA Leagues

I'm not sure if lines people are allowed in the league, but I know that it's at least frowned upon, so refer to flex league. The advantage you have here is your teammates can help you confirm if you are right about calls, even though by rule they cannot give voice to this in the match, they have absolutely no say so, and it can escalate the situation when people outside the court interject themselves into the match. What they can do is give you a nod yes or no to confirm that that call was correct or not, reaffirming or reassuring you. As a teammate when you can reassure your teammate that indeed the other team is making good calls, then you can help keep the peace.

Bottom line, be wise, don't get ripped off, but use the best in diplomacy to resolve the situation and these problems can be rectified, and the truth of the opposition's and your character can come to light.

Be the bigger person.

Chapter Forty

Why Should I Be A Tennis Citizen?

"This is the way." ~ The Mandolorian

The great news is that many people have begun playing tennis during and in the post-Covid-19 world. Tennis is one of the safest sports both for potential injury, improving longevity, and reducing the risk of spreading disease. The USTA commissioned a study, finding that the tennis ball does not make a good transmitter for illnesses. The bad news is that not all of the new players have been trained in court etiquette.

The ultimate goal is to be as helpful as is useful, mitigate annoyances and distractions for yourself and others. Being known as a polite player is a great distinction.

How you enter the court, retrieve the ball, when and how you send it back, what are the unwritten rules of tennis, we will cover those things. In reality, they are written, but fewer people read "The Code" these days. Etiquette is somewhat of transmission by way of oral history.   Align yourself with these things, and you will find that your tennis flows, but if you are a major violator on one or more counts, then you might get some less than ideal reactions from those who know better.

Entering and Crossing Courts

Let's start from the beginning.   In most places, court times are limited. Stay within your allotted time, unless of course, no one is around to be bothered. Whether you are at a club, park, homeowners association, or private court, know the rules and abide by them. Commonly, players will blindly stay on the court, when another person or group has it reserved. If someone has that court reserved for 10 am, then you should be off the court at 9:59 am, so that they can walk on and have their full time. What makes anyone think they should still be on the court one second into someone else's court time?   Of course, if it's your buddy, and everyone is low-key, that's another thing. As far as I am concerned, I am going to obey the letter of the law on this one, for the greater good. Don't be the kid who says, "One more game", or "Let us finish our set".

It's unsettling when you have a court invader.

It's too bad you didn't finish your set earlier, but that does not give you a license to take up precious time. In some places, you can only get one hour of play before you are off, so waiting 5 to 10 more minutes is a strong imposition. There might be different rules for singles and doubles.   Another thing you can do is arrive before your time, and with 5 minutes left before your time, gently inform those players that you have that court at the top of the hour.   Then walk boldly in at the moment the clock strikes. Of course, if you have to cross a court to get to your court, make sure you do so in between points being played on the court or courts you have to cross. In that case, you might want to start your court crossing two minutes early. The ideal time to cross is on a changeover, the second-best is between games, but if a point has ended, if you get the attention of a player on that court and ask, "May I cross, 99% of the time they will say yes", but they might ask you to wait until after the next point.

Ball Management

There are general rules for retrieving and asking for balls to be retrieved, then there are some exceptions to those rules. It's all based on what is most convenient for the other players, what the general expectation is in the sport, and what is most expedient. I hope to make this as clear and simple as possible.

Your Ball On Their Court

When your ball rolls onto another court, resist the urge to run onto the other person's court. First stop, look and listen. Look to see if they are playing a point, and/or if they stopped their point because the ball rolled across making it dangerous or a visual distraction. Once you see that they have stopped the point, then look to see if they are automatically going to get your ball. It may have gone unnoticed in the corner of their court. There is a certain shorthand in how to request it. "Ball Please?" With a gentle point to the ball if they don't see it. Also, look to see if both players at the end of their point are way out of position to go get it, if you are much closer, then it's easier to go get it. If both players are on a changeover, and your ball went all the way to the far corner, ask "May I?", and the obvious answer is yes. The main point here being that you want to show deference to the wishes of the people on that court. When I am teaching tennis, I don't want strangers to my student running on the court, so I retrieve many balls for them.

When A Ball Comes On To Your Court

You are responsible to return it, but not in the middle of a point. Those people should not come onto your court without your permission. If a ball rolls onto your court in the playing area, automatically stop, and play a let. Of course, if the player was hitting an un-returnable shot at the same moment as the ball rolling on, then the point may stand. Use your best judgment, and don't be trivial with the rules.

When you get the ball, again, stop, look, and listen. Get the position of the ball, then look to see which player wants it. It could be the server way on the other side, or it could be the returner near you. Send it to the closest player who requests it, but do not send it to the nearest player if they direct you to get it to the server. The Code says that you should return the ball to them on one bounce, but a nice roll of the ball also works well. You don't want to hit it hrd, or make them have to move to get the ball, if so, that's time for a brief, polite apology. It's not a big deal, but you don't want to inconvenience them. Stuff happens, but do the best you can.

Whatever you do, don't disturb anyone who is in the middle of a point, don't stand close to their court creating a visual distraction for one or both players. You can wait a minute if they have a super long rally. Another exception is when you see that your ball is dangerous to them, and neither player takes notice, that's when safety comes first and you say with some level of urgency, "Ball on!", because the worst thing that could happen is that they stop on the ball, break their ankle or fall on their head and you didn't warn them. So, yes, it can be that serious.

You want to find a 'Friend At Court'
that includes The Code.

Every once in a while you find a weirdo who hits the balls into the corners away from you, hangs their towel at the net on the opposite fence at eye level to distract you, doesn't get the ball back to you on one bounce, etc. Be sure to educate that person, with kindness.

Every Point Ends With A Point Won

If there is a let, the point has not ended, but in all other cases, someone will win or lose the point. If someone is not sure of the call, you don't play the point over. If they aren't sure, then the call is 'Good Shot', that's a rule of tennis. Alternatives might seem kind and nice, but they are not tennis. The assumption is that it goes both ways. When a player calls the ball out in error and realizes their mistake, it doesn't matter if they hit the ball back in, the point is over and they lose it. There used to be a rule that if they hit the ball back in after an errant call, then the point would be played over, but a small lunatic fringe of weirdos was using that as a license to call balls out with no penalty.

The whole point of the rules and etiquette is that it makes for a peaceful fun match played inside the rules, then everyone can cope with the outcome, but when people use gamesmanship, rudeness, and awkwardness to win, you probably won't be friends moving forward. You may find that as the positivity reaches a peak, the level of play also goes up and everyone has fun. A rising tide of enjoyment raises all boats.

Chapter Forty One

What's Next On The Strategy Menu?

One of the biggest problems new players face is that they have no one to play. You are responsible to solve this problem, as there are not many people who will help you with this. If you have a coach or pro, that you work with, they can help you with player matching, or how to find a game, and if they don't, then they are not a very good help.

About 80% of people who play tennis simply want to rally for30-45 minutes, get their heart rate up, go home, and do chores.

About 15% of people want to play a social set of doubles or maybe singles.

The lunatic fringe of under 5% of people want to play competitively winner take all, no holds barred. Our systems of play usually force people into a mold they do not prefer.

Public Park 'In Crowds' How To Get Inside

One thing you can do is find the local parks, where tennis is played. Look for a time when the most people are around, usually Saturday or Sunday mornings or midweek after work. Go and make friends. Express your love of the game. If they have a hitting wall, hit on it, until someone asks if you want to hit. Sometimes you can have a 5-10 minute hitting session with someone who is about to leave, and that is the beginning of your tennis journey. Park Tennis is similar to the Viet Nam War, in that no one engaged with new soldiers until they have survived 6 weeks because a large percentage were killed right away. Be a survivor, keep going to the court for weeks at a time at the same time, then people will see that you are not just a one time interloper. You will have to show a fairly high level of determination at the park, but at a club, it can be much easier because there is a captive audience. even so, some tennis coaches are more helpful than others.

Rally Or Die

It's pretty simple, that in the transaction of adding value to another, you have to hold up your end of the bargain. People generally will regularly play with people who can rally, challenge them a little, and are on a similar level. If you can't rally, or they can't rally with you, or you are a loose cannon, with not enough control, they won't want to play with you. It's that simple.

If you can rally, people will want to play with you.

There is an unwritten rule: if you are rallying you will hit a few friendly shots, before going for an aggressive one. If you feed winners past your partner, regularly, they are not going to be your partner much longer. Don't give up, just consult your local tennis coach, and work on the ability to keep the ball going a bit longer, and then you will be the one who everyone wants to hit the ball, with all day long, or until it's time for a frosty beverage.

Tennis Is Being Played Differently

About 20 years ago, most players played tournaments, then that shifted, and most people played on USTA Teams, but these days there is a massive proliferation of differing playing outlets. Flex leagues, under various brands, are becoming very popular, both because you get to play singles, play often, and the scheduling is more flexible.

Tournaments often have scheduling problems, so take it in stride. Sadly, some of them are very poorly planned, so when you sign up for one be sure you know what you are getting into, as many tournament directors can be very poor at communicating, so try them out early, see how quickly you can get a response to an email, call or text.

Being A Good Flex League Citizen

If you play a flex league and you have 8 different opponents, I can assure you that you can make one or two new friends out of that group, who are close enough in ability and enjoyable enough to hang out with that you may end up playing and practicing often. You may meet 5 or 6 civil players, and you may agree to play again outside of the league. Then there is a good chance that 1 or 2, that could be difficult or eccentric personalities. Bear with it as that can make for great stories, later at cocktail parties, and/or you will wish not to see them again. The worst I have heard is that someone brought their not so friendly pit-bull to a match.   Don't play a match if you don't feel safe. It's not worth it. So when they call or text you to play again you say something like "I have to wash my hamster", or "I'm baking cookies for a wedding shower", they will get the hint.

There are a lot of emerging brands of flex leagues being played today, and if someone were to sponsor this book, I will gladly promote a particular brand. Put in your favorite search engine "Flex Leagues Near Me"

About The Author

Bill Patton is a 30+ Year Tennis Professional, Founder of BrainSports.Coach a neuroscience outlet for coach, parent and athlete. Coach Patton is a Senior Contributor to SportsEdTV.com, and regularly contributes to Tennis Business Newsletter. He has written 13 books, 7 now in print. He is available over video call for one on one coaching, and in person at Sequoyah Country Club in Oakland, CA. You can reach out to him at infinitevisioncoach@gmail.com.

BrainSports.Coach